Papal Power

Papal Power
Its Origins and Development

Henry T. Hudson

The Trinity Foundation

Papal Power
Its Origin and Development

First edition copyright © 1981
Henry T. Hudson

Second edition copyright © 1989
Henry T. Hudson

Third edition copyright © 2008
The Trinity Foundation
Post Office Box 68
Unicoi, Tennessee 37692
www.trinityfoundation.org
423.743.0199

ISBN-10: 1-891777-25-4
ISBN-13: 978-1-891777-25-7

DEDICATION

To all my beloved Italian friends who know
better than I could ever know what it is
like to live *sotto i Papi*.

Preface

THE twentieth century saw the emergence of some of the most bloody totalitarian regimes of the second millennium after Christ: the Nazi regime in Germany, which lasted only 12 years but has received the most attention from historians; the Leninist regime in the Soviet Union, which lasted 84 years, and its deepest secrets are still unknown and now being hidden by a resurgent secret police state; the Maoist regime in China, which has now remained in power for nearly 60 years, and has probably killed more people than the Hitler and Lenin regimes together. Then there are the lesser dictatorships such as Cuba, Cambodia, the Congo, Sudan, and Vietnam.

These regimes did not suddenly arise from a vacuum, nor did they spring full-grown from the brow of Zeus. They had roots – political, religious, and ideological roots – that connect them to earlier and even more profound forms of totalitarianism. What the historians of totalitarianism in the twentieth century have largely missed is the connections between the modern regimes and a very ancient institution, the Roman Catholic Church-State, which existed for centuries – by far the longest surviving, the most intellectually sophisticated, and the most globally dispersed form of totalitarianism. They missed this connection because the twentieth-century historians were largely secularists who did not believe that theology plays any major role in modern world affairs. Perhaps, they thought, theology was a major factor in world affairs a thousand years ago, but since we have all become Enlightened, it plays little or no role, and it can be safely ignored. This enormous blind spot in their thinking has caused modern historians to miss the many connections between Romanism and modern totalitarianism.

Long before the early nineteenth-century German philosopher G. W. F. Hegel, who is frequently credited or blamed for the emergence of modern totalitarianism, said that the State is God walking on Earth, the popes had claimed that the Roman Church, as represented by the pope, was God walking on Earth. When the pope spoke, God was speaking. When he spoke, he was infallible. When he spoke, all men, not just priests or Roman Catholics, owed instant and entire obedience. No person or institution has ever made more arrogant claims than this. Hitler claimed to speak for *das Volk*; Lenin claimed to speak for the People, but the popes have claimed to speak for God. They are the "Supreme Pontiffs," the bridges between Heaven and Earth. Their rule is absolute and complete. They not only have power over the living, but over the dead as well, remitting and imposing punishment on them in this life and the next.

Henry Hudson's monograph on the origins and development of papal power fills a gap in modern historiography and is an excellent introduction to a study of the connections between Romanist and modern totalitarianism. He is not laboring under the delusion of so many historians that theology does not influence world affairs. He recognizes that ideas rule the world, and that the most potent ideas are and will always be theological ideas, for they concern the most important questions that human beings can ask.

John W. Robbins
October 2007

Contents

CONTENTS

Foreword

"THE best pope is the worst pope," affirmed Luther with regard to the papal institution, upon which rests the government of the Roman Catholic Church.

Luther's affirmation is not an expression of the Reformer's personal opinion with regard to the person or conduct of one of the Roman pontiffs, but the expression of a radical judgment of condemnation upon the papal institution itself, an institution which, in its form and in its character, is not based on any apparent instruction in the Scriptures, but rather is in open contrast with them. For Luther, involved as he was in recalling Christendom to a rediscovery of the Word of God as being the one and only authority in matters of faith and conduct, this contrast was more than sufficient for him to express severe condemnation of the papacy.

Many evangelical believers of our time no longer seem to hold a similar consistent view of the relation between the Scriptures, faith, and knowledge. For this reason, the evangelicals of our time can best be described as having but "little power" (*Revelation* 3:8), barely sufficient to carry forward in some way the mandate of evangelization, but not sufficient to put to the test "them who say they are apostles, and are not," and to find them liars (*Revelation* 2:2).

In times like these, I am delighted with the decision of Dr.

Henry T. Hudson, to write and to publish a work on the origins and the development of papal power.

When the television charisma and the public relations of the present Roman pontiff appear to exercise an influence over the convictions and the sentiments of so many evangelical believers, particularly in the United States (an influence seemingly more persuasive than that exercised by the Scriptures), it is providential that a book such as this should seek to make known the history and the nature of the papal institution in the light of the Scriptures.

Evangelicals cannot do less than lay hold of such knowledge, if they want to accept in earnest the responsibility to communicate the liberating power of the Gospel "first" to Roman Catholics, "and also" to everyone else (*Romans* 1:16). Moreover, this knowledge will have the beneficial effect of protecting the evangelical churches from the peril of producing, or of listening to, leaders who are not completely submissive to the authority of the Word of God. Even if the awakening of the Reformation has been, and is, a vaccine remarkably effective in the face of papal tendencies, the danger of the reappearance of this sickness in other more extenuating forms is ever present.

I believe that the labor of Dr. Hudson has been determined not only by his love for the truth, but also by the love which he has for the believers and the people of Italy, whose lot it is to live under the nefarious influence of the Vatican City-State and its king.

For this affection toward the people of my country, I want to thank Dr. Hudson, and I want to assure him that in the hearts of the Italian evangelical believers there has always been a particular place for all those who, like him, have understood and sought to share the implications of the duty entrusted to us by God to proclaim and to live the Gospel in this country.

Elio Milazzo
President, Italian Evangelical Alliance
Florence, Italy

Introduction

"JOHN PAUL SUPERSTAR." So read the front cover of *Time* magazine dated October 15, 1979. Journalistic exaggeration? Perhaps, but to judge from the television coverage and the public printed news media, the impression was given that the greater part of the population of the United States had turned to Roman Catholicism during the first week of October 1979. By any earthly standards, the pope's visit was a smash hit! He spoke before the United Nations. He captured nationwide television coverage. He was honored with a White House reception and a private meeting with President Jimmy Carter, a Southern Baptist, and his family. Senator Ted Kennedy did not hesitate to kiss his ring in public. Headlines such as "JEWS AND PROTESTANTS LAUD VISIT" appeared in major newspapers. David Sanford, managing editor of *Harper's*, wrote "It was a collective act unrivalled in the annals of crowd psychology since the Beatles...." In a footnote Sanford expanded this observation with the somewhat facetious comment: "The pope is more popular than the Beatles, who, according to John Lennon, were more popular than Jesus; where this leaves Jesus is not clear."[1] Moreover, before concluding, he exclaimed, "I cannot remember a news event in which so much that was

1. David Sanford, "The Pope's Groupies," *Harper's*, December 1979, 86.

said and written by professional journalists contained so much puffery."[2]

The phenomenon of the pope's visit will no doubt provide much fuel for psycho-sociological analysis for some time to come. How can anyone begin to explain his widespread popular reception? Whatever happened to the traditional anti-papal sentiments common in American history? The early colonists and the Founding Fathers were predominantly progeny from Reformed Protestantism.[3] By and large they were outspokenly anti-papal. This propensity was evident throughout the nineteenth, and on into the twentieth century. What then brought about the change? Perhaps one reporter came closer to the answer than he realized when he wrote, "Nobody is prejudiced any more because nobody takes [religion] that seriously; you have to believe in something first to be bigoted."[4] Be all this as it may, I found it to be no small coincidence that the commotion connected with the pope's visit should take place at the same time that I began looking over my manuscript for this book. However, this was by no means the main reason for the interest in my subject, although I must admit it spurred my desire to see the result of my research published and presented to a wider audience.

Living in Rome

My initial interest in studying the origins and development of papal power reaches back at least two decades to the several years of my life spent in Italy. The experiences which derive

2. David Sanford, *Harper's*, 89.

3. Loraine Boettner estimated that approximately two-thirds of the entire population prior to 1776 was Reformed Protestant (Loraine Boettner, *The Reformed Doctrine of Predestination*, 1974, 382-383).

4. David Sanford, *Harper's*, 88.

from living there – that is, actually residing among the Italian people, going about the normal daily routines of life in much the way they would – produce an altogether different diary of observations and impressions from that which might be reported by any two-week-overnight-turned-expert tourist. In this regard, the words of Luigi Barzini are pungent. He wrote, "The Italian way of life cannot be considered a success except by temporary visitors. It solves no problems. It makes them worse."[5] In fact, not only do "temporary visitors" tend to misread the complex cultural expressions of life in Italy, but I have also noticed that they sometimes are among the first to object to any first-hand insights that might be shared. That in itself is a key to the enigmatical nature of the Italian way of life. Superficiality and reality become easily confused. "Unless you live there," wrote Morris West, "it is impossible to believe how crazy the country can be, how precarious are the foundations upon which it rests."[6]

West, while writing on a subject different from the one which interests me, nevertheless includes among the foundations of

5. Luigi Barzini, *The Italians*, 1965, 339. The quotation from Barzini comes in his concluding paragraph. Barzini has another observation three pages earlier, which relates directly to this point: "Foreign visitors are fascinated. They are won over, as they have always been, by the 'charm of Italy.' Italian life is gay, effervescent, intoxicating. The *dolce vita* looks now more *dolce* than it ever was. Very few travelers see the ugliness underneath, the humiliation, the suffering. Not one in a hundred perceives the fundamental dreariness of everything under the glittering ormolu, the bitter fate of men who are condemned perennially to amuse themselves and the world, to hide their innermost feelings, to be *simpatici* at all costs in order to make a living. What do they know of the peculiar feeling of frustration and resigned discontent which paralyses the best Italians?" (336).

6. Morris West, "Terror as an Historical Inheritance," *Esquire*, April 25, 1978, 77.

modern Italy an inheritance of stupidity built into the system by – among other historical forces – "absolutist popes." Most assuredly, the Italy of yesterday and the Italy of today cannot be appreciated in any fair degree without some reference to the pervasive power of the papacy. The longer I lived there, and the more I came to understand the various facets of the overall culture, the more I began to realize just how extensive was this power. That such a condition does prevail is not difficult to comprehend. The papacy, as most people are well aware, is the governing body of the Roman Catholic Church, and according to a number of religious census statistics, more than ninety-four per cent of the Italian population belongs to that church.

Some form of personal relationship with the Roman Church is almost indispensable for survival and success in Italy. This might seem like a sweeping generalization, but Barzini, discussing the role of organizational structures that promote security and advancement in Italian society, began with the church, "the oldest and largest of all…a State within a State…" He described the "holy Roman Catholic Church" as "the greatest flowering of the Italian political genius." So pervasive is the influence of this enormous religio-political organization in the life of an average Italian that, "It can accompany him, step by step, from birth to death, assuring him a good job and a steady career, protecting him from the envy of rivals, procuring for him, at times, worldly success, fame, political power, and wealth."[7]

In all likelihood, some readers will do little more than blink over such observations. However, because I know by immediate

7. Barzini, *The Italians*, 220, 304.

18

involvement something of the frustrations of life in Italy, I cannot help but be troubled by them. For me, they bear disturbing implications. For example, how do I reconcile what is taught in the Bible about the social impact of the Christian faith upon any given society and the quality of life in Italy? Admittedly, a similar question might be raised with reference to any other land where the Christian church has a solid foothold. But is there any other nation, which can boast a church membership of ninety-four per cent of the population?

Religion and Society

The Roman Catholic Church claims to be the true Church of Christ upon the Earth, and the pope believes himself to be the actual vicar of Jesus Christ.[8] Imagine what a Muslim or a

8. On June 29, 2007, the "Supreme Pontiff," Benedict XVI, ratified and confirmed answers given by the Congregation for the Doctrine of the Faith to questions regarding certain aspects of the Roman Catholic Doctrine of the Church.

In these answers Benedict XVI affirmed that, "The Second Vatican Council neither changed nor intended to change this doctrine; rather it developed, deepened, and more fully explained it. This was exactly what John XXIII said at the beginning of the Council. [Address of October 11, 1962: "The Council…wishes to transmit Catholic doctrine, whole and entire, without alteration or deviation…this certain and immutable doctrine…"]. Paul VI affirmed it and commented in the act of promulgating the Constitution *Lumen Gentium*: "There is no better comment to make than to say that this promulgation really changes nothing of the traditional doctrines."

In response to a second question, the Congregation and Benedict XVI wrote that "Christ 'established here on Earth' only one Church and instituted it as a 'visible and spiritual community'…. This Church…subsists in the Catholic Church, governed by the successor of Peter and the Bishops in communion with him."

In response to the last question, "Why do the texts of the Council, and those of the Magisterium since the Council, not use the title 'Church' with

Buddhist might think about Christianity, should they happen to be direct observers of Italian life! Would they have any way of knowing that visible ecclesiastical power and true Christianity are not one and the same thing? Yet who could really fault them, should they entertain the notion that there is some cause-and-effect relationship between the power and influence of the Roman Church and the Italian way of life? Certainly, such a judgment is frequently made by Western minds with regard to Muslim countries where similar percentages prevail. Why not here? At best, the influence of the Roman Church for the betterment of the Italian people is negligible, and at worst, it may well be a direct contributor to the debilitating impossibilities of their daily frustrations. This latter alternative has been ably argued by a number of qualified observers, beginning as early as Machiavelli. What is more, there have been those who, having at one time been fervent Roman Catholics, have nevertheless been led to view the Roman Church as "the antithesis of Christianity."[9]

---

regard to those Christian Communities born out of the Reformation of the sixteenth century?" The Congregation and Benedict XVI answered: "According to Catholic Doctrine, these Communities do not enjoy apostolic succession in the Sacrament of Orders, and are, therefore, deprived of a constitutive element of the Church. These ecclesial communities which, superficially because of the absence of the sacramental priesthood, have not preserved the genuine and integral substance of the Eucharistic Mystery cannot, according to Catholic Doctrine, be called 'Churches' in the proper sense."

In short, the second Vatican Council did not change the Roman Catholic doctrine of the Church, and there is only one genuine Church on Earth, the Roman Catholic Church. – *Editor*.

[9.] Alexander Robertson, *The Roman Catholic Church in Italy*, 1904, 88. Most theological libraries possess a wide assortment of authors, beginning particularly from Luther's time, who have experienced such a change of mind.

Of course, there is always the question as to the actual extent of the influence of religion upon any given society. And, admittedly, that is not easy to measure. However, quite frankly, I believe only a prejudiced fool, or perhaps one blinded by the reflex of modern secularism, would want to argue that there is absolutely no correlation. One need only think of events in Iran during 1979 to recognize that my language is anything but exaggerated. The *de facto* ruler, and the power behind the Muslim forces which overthrew the Shah, was the leading Shi-ite ayatollah, Ruholla Khomeini. If anything, American foreign policy failed to face up to the effective force of religion in Iran.

Any number of reputable scholars could be cited who accept the assumption that religion can and does in effect produce a distinctive outlook on life. Two well-known examples in this regard, would be the sociological studies of Max Weber and R. H. Tawney.[10] Also, while not in the same category as these two studies, the observations of Alexis de Tocqueville are worthy of consideration. De Tocqueville wrote in the early half of the nineteenth century, and some of the things he observed with reference to the differences between religion in his native France and that of America serve well to illustrate what I am trying to say: for example, the distinction he made between a "barren, traditional faith which seems to vegetate" and that which lives in the soul.[11] He saw quite clearly, even as the Holy Scriptures so patently declare, that there is a world of difference between mere formalism in religion and the dynamic influence of sincere faith in God (*Matthew* 15:7-9; 23:1-33).

10. Max Weber, *The Protestant Ethic and the Spirit of Capitalism* [1904-1905] 1930; and R. H. Tawney, *Religion and the Rise of Capitalism*, 1963.
11. Alexis de Tocqueville, *Democracy in America* [1835-1840] 1945; Volume 1, 317.

Perhaps I ought to mention the fact that De Tocqueville was a member of the Roman Catholic Church. His observations, therefore, can scarcely be discounted as those of a biased antagonist. If anything, they come across with greater significance. With this in mind, I would like to call attention to two other observations, which bear upon the point that I am trying to make. First, after acknowledging that the greatest part of British America had been peopled by men who had shaken off the authority of the pope, De Tocqueville told his readers that in America, in contrast to the way it was in France, the spirit of religion and the spirit of freedom marched together in close accord. By implication, his expression of astonishment at this phenomenon reveals more to a perceptive reader than does his proffered explanation. However, in his explanation – and this is the second observation – he traced the cause to the principle of separation of church and state. Obviously, from his remarks, he considered this "new state of things" to be a great blessing.[12] In other words, De Tocqueville was persuaded that nothing but detrimental consequences can follow in any society where religion is permitted to be prostituted to further political ends.

Vatican City

But I am drifting slightly off my subject. Let me return to what prompted this study in the first place. So far, in essence, what I have suggested is that during my residence in Italy I was disturbed by a disconcerting paradox. On the one hand, there was a powerful ecclesiastical system permeating most facets of Italian society and supposedly representing the church of Christ upon Earth, and on the other hand, a

12. *Democracy in America*, I, 311, 319, 322, *et passim*.

quality of life, which appeared to contradict so much of that for which Christianity stands. Were my sentiments totally without reason? Had not the Lord Jesus Christ himself said, "A good tree cannot bring forth evil fruit....Wherefore by their fruits you shall know them" (*Matthew* 7:18, 20)? But beyond this disquieting inconsistency, there was one further matter that prodded me in the direction of a study dealing with the origins and growth of papal power. It was the enormity of papal power itself. And, in certain respects, this particular question bothered me more than the paradox I have already described.

In very obvious ways, the enormity and power of the papacy are more apparent in the city of Rome than possibly in any other place in the world. This fact becomes particularly noticeable when one visits St. Peter's Basilica and Vatican City. I would suppose that I have visited the so-called papal state (a land area of just over 100 acres) at least a dozen times. Most of these visits were made at the request of friends who had enlisted my services as a kind of tour guide to help direct them through what are unquestionably some of the most beautiful artistic masterpieces in the world. Who, with any degree of aesthetic taste, could fail to appreciate the breathtaking marvels crowded within the five-mile labyrinth of buildings, which houses no less than thirteen museums? Little wonder the faces of the tourists reflect the agog state of their minds. They are walking through corridor after corridor of priceless art exhibits. In certain respects, I myself am no different. Every time I have viewed the Vatican art treasures, I have sensed inexpressible wonderment. This is especially true when my eyes try to take in what is probably the centerpiece of all, Michelangelo's work on the ceiling of the Sistine Chapel.

However, my own appreciation has always been tempered by mixed emotions. On almost every occasion, particularly as I walked around the inside of St. Peter's Basilica, my soul has been troubled by a single question. In order to grasp the force of the question, it is perhaps necessary to try to imagine the scene. I am standing somewhere in the central nave near Bernini's massive canopy which covers the papal altar. From this vantage point, I can have a comprehensive view of much which makes up the grandeur of the largest church building in Christendom. Also from this same position, I can better observe the thousands of people who are milling around. For example, there is the seemingly endless line of people close by who are waiting to touch or to kiss the extended toe of a black marble statue of Peter. Countless millions have performed this act of veneration, and the features of the toes have been virtually worn away. As my eyes take in all that is before me, my mind begins to ponder the question: How can anyone relate all this to that which is set forth in the pages of the New Testament? Were I to go through the crowds asking individuals this question, I would no doubt elicit a variety of responses, but on the whole, I would think that few would sympathize with my implied skepticism. As far as the majority appears to be concerned, I would venture to say that they harbor little, if any, doubt about a direct relationship between what they see and the basic teachings of Christianity. Of course, for most Italian Roman Catholics, it could hardly be otherwise. What they see has, in their minds, always been coterminous with Christianity. Furthermore, on the whole, they possess little, if any, first-hand knowledge of the content of Holy Scripture. This also could hardly be otherwise, since it has been, until only very recently, the consistent policy of the papal hierarchy to oppose the reading and study of the Bible, by both priests and laity.[13]

This then, the wide disparity between the straightforward teachings of the New Testament and the greatness and grandeur of the Roman Church, became the cause of no small irritation to me. I felt sure that some kind of rational explanation to the phenomenon could be found. My academic background in both history and theology gave me reason to believe that I could find it. My opinion that there had to be some causative relationship between the centuries-long dominating influence of the Roman Church and the "frustration and resigned discontent" of the Italian people was another matter.[14] Limitations of time and ability precluded my becoming involved in such a comprehensive field of study. So, leaving this latter problem, I took up the former and, spurred primarily by the question of the incredible gap between Holy Scripture and Roman papal traditions, I began my research. Did I bridge the gap? The following pages, for what they might be worth, contain the answer.

13. One need only call to mind the words of Signor Guiseppe Zanardelli, Premier of Italy at the beginning of the twentieth century, in order to appreciate the profound significance of this point: "Woe to the Roman Catholic Church when my countrymen get hold of the Old and New Testaments; then they will know the difference between Jesus Christ and his so-called vicar" (Robertson, *The Roman Catholic Church in Italy,* 225).

14. Barzini, *The Italians,* 336.

2

The Origins of Papal Power

THE question of origins can be a very complicated matter. However, according to the traditions of Roman Catholic dogma, the source of papal power is traceable directly to Holy Scripture. An almost endless array of literary sources, particularly during the Middle Ages, could be cited in support of this claim. In effect, what this means is that the papal institution has been able to associate itself in an apparently inextricable way with divine authority. In such a context, papal power becomes nothing short of the practical outworking of doctrinal concepts based upon sacred Scripture. If one should ask for a specific Scriptural example to illustrate the association, in all likelihood *Matthew* 16:18-19 would be given. Without any doubt, in this regard, this is the most quoted Biblical passage of all. Proof of its importance becomes very evident to tourists visiting St. Peter's Basilica in Rome. As they stand by the papal altar in the central nave and look up to admire Michelangelo's magnificent dome, they cannot fail to note the bold inscription around the base: "*Tu es Petrus, et super hanc petram aedificabo ecclesiam meam, et tibi dabo claves regni coelorum.*" ("You are Peter, and upon this rock I will build my Church, and I will give unto you the keys of the kingdom of Heaven.")

Who – or What – Is the Rock?

"From these words," according to Wladimir D'Ormesson, "the Papacy was born. They were to remain its basic charter through the centuries."[1] By inference, the words were repeatedly proffered in support of two fundamental propositions: (1) Peter, as the rock upon whom the Church would be built, was granted authoritative jurisdiction over all the followers of Jesus Christ; and (2) by what is known as "apostolic succession," those who succeed Peter become the inheritors of this universal authority. Where is Rome mentioned in this text? Of course, it is not; but then it need not be, for the primacy of the Roman bishopric is derived from the claim that Peter was Bishop of Rome, and remained such till his death.[2]

1. Wladimir D'Ormesson, *The Papacy*, translated by Michael Derrick; Volume 81 of the *Twentieth Century Encyclopedia of Catholicism*, edited by Henri Daniel Rops, 1959, 10.

2. Wladimir D'Ormesson considers Peter's presence at Rome to be crucial with respect to the founding of the papacy (27). Protestant champions have attempted to prove that Peter never was at Rome. If it is possible to prove a negative at all, then it may be concluded, at least with a high degree of probability, that he was not at Rome during any of the time covered by the history of the canonical Scriptures. He may have suffered martyrdom at Rome, but the tradition-legend of a twenty-five year episcopate can hardly be maintained unless, of course, he was an absentee bishop. The traditional dates for his episcopate are from A.D. 41 to 66. Consider the following facts:

In 44 he was imprisoned in Jerusalem (*Acts* 12).

In 52 he was at the Council of Jerusalem (*Acts* 15).

In 53 Paul joined him at Antioch (*Galatians* 2).

In 58 Paul wrote to the Romans, but does not mention him. In *Romans* 1:11, he wants to impart special gifts, and in *Romans* 1:15 he is ready to preach there. He sends greetings to twenty-seven persons, but none to Peter.

In 61 Paul is conveyed a prisoner to Rome, and certain brethren go to meet him, but not Peter.

Granted the premises, the arguments for what has become known as "the Petrine theory" are easy to follow. Those who succeed in the Bishopric of Rome are the rightful heirs of Peter and therefore inherit the universal jurisdiction over the whole Christian church. There is, however, as any thoughtful person will quickly recognize, a wide gap between the words of *Matthew* 16:18 and the premises and deductions of Roman Catholic doctrine.

The literature produced by various exegetical studies of *Matthew* 16:18 is enormous.[3] That such should be the case is

---

At Rome Paul writes to the Galatians, and mentions Peter, but not as being there or as having been pontiff there for twenty years.

The *Epistles* to the *Ephesians, Philippians, Colossians,* and *Philemon* were all written from Rome; but while others are mentioned as sending messages, or as being associated with Paul, Peter is never once mentioned.

From Rome also Paul's last letter is written (the *Second Epistle to Timothy*). He says, "At my first answer no man stood with me, but all men forsook me" (2 *Timothy* 4:16). If Peter were Bishop of Rome he enjoyed an immunity not accorded to Paul, and he is guilty of having forsaken the great apostle.

And, finally, in this very *Epistle,* written from Rome immediately before his martyrdom, Paul says, "Only Luke is with me" (2 *Timothy* 4:11). This is conclusive.

So Paul had written to Rome, he had been in Rome, and at the end he writes from Rome, and not only never once mentions Peter, but also declares, "Only Luke is with me." Peter is simply not there.

3. The text of *Matthew* 16:18 is controverted over the interpretation of the Greek words *petros* and *petra.* An interlinear transliteration might be given as follows:

Su ei Petros, kai epi taute te petra
You are Peter, and upon this the rock
oikodomeso mou ten ekklesian.
I will build of me the church.

A simple straightforward consideration of the grammatical construction seems to rule out Peter as the *petra.* We might paraphrase the text:

not hard to understand, since so much is at stake as far as papal claims to universal power are concerned. Among the early commentaries of the church fathers there was great diversity of opinion over the precise identity of the rock upon which the church would be built. One study made by the French Roman Catholic Launoy revealed the following facts: Seventeen of the patristic writers said that Peter was the rock; forty-four were of the opinion that it was Peter's faith; sixteen favored the view that the rock was Christ; and eight said that it referred to all the apostles.[4] From those early writers, up till today, the interpretation of *Matthew* 16:18 has remained a major bone of contention.

During the Middle Ages, particularly the twelfth and thirteenth centuries, canon lawyers followed the "well-worn grooves of patristic controversy in discussing the precise connotation of *super honc petram*."[5] If there was any shift in emphasis it was in the fact that the church was built principally upon Christ, and secondarily upon Peter. Differences of opinion were of no great consequence, since it was sufficient that the words of *Matthew* 16:18 at least permitted Peter some position of special importance. By this time in history, the whole Petrine theory was so well established that the mere fact of Peter's prominence constituted adequate evidence to support the theory. In later centuries, scholars might highlight the apparent logical fallacy, which unwittingly reads the con-

---

"You are Peter, a movable stone, but upon this, the immovable rock, I will build my church...."

The theological implications of making Peter "the immovable rock" would seem to be of serious consequences in the light of the context and Peter's later life. See *Matthew* 16:23; 26:69-75.

4. Cited in George Salmon, *The Infallibility of the Church*, 1914, 335.

5. Brian Tierney, *Foundations of the Conciliar Theory*, 1955, 25.

clusion into the premise, but in the historical circumstances of the Middle Ages this was hardly possible. Papal power was *de facto* a reality. *Matthew* 16:18 provided a kind of divine cornerstone to the reality.

Thus, while the Petrine theory was inseparably associated with *Matthew* 16:18, it was not necessarily dependent upon the identification of Peter with the rock. For example, there were theologians such as Gabriel Biel who, as late as the fifteenth century, while yielding obedience to papal authority, nevertheless interpreted the rock to be Christ.[6] Incidentally, we might mention in passing that there have been Protestant expositors also who have opted for Peter's being the rock.[7] Obviously, then, the equation of Peter with the rock was not the equivalent of accepting papal views of power. However, as far as papal supporters were concerned, they were content merely to derive from Christ's words special eminence for Peter, which in itself tended to undergird the whole papal structure with great dignity and divine authority.

Apostolic Succession

The controversy concerning the true identification of the rock, as important as it might be, should not be allowed to eclipse inquiry concerning the second proposition upon which the papacy stands, namely, the theory of apostolic suc-

---

6. Heiko A. Oberman, *The Harvest of Medieval Theology*, 1963, 413.

7. William Smith, *Dictionary of the Bible,* 4 volumes, 1870; Volume III, 24-48. See also Alfred Plummer, *An Exegetical Commentary of the Gospel of Matthew*, 228-229; William L. Pettingil, *The Gospel of the Kingdom*, 203; Alfred Barnes, *An Explanatory and Practical Commentary on Matthew*, 170; John D. Davis, *The Westminster Dictionary of the Bible*, 473; James Hastings, *Dictionary of the Bible*, article on "Peter;" Oscar Cullman, *Peter*, 206-207; Marvin R. Vincent, *Word Studies in the New Testament*, Volume 1, 91-92.

cession. Does *Matthew* 16:18 support the claim that there was to be a perpetuation of authority and jurisdiction over the universal church through the line of Bishops whose bishopric was located at Rome?[8] At the risk of sounding facetious, we would say that any affirmative answer to this question would indicate an extraordinary mode of exegesis. Obviously, no objective examination of the words could ever support the notion. Besides, the whole idea of universal authority, let alone apostolic succession, was far from accepted even some 600 years after the Lord spoke the words to Peter. Gregory the Great, "servant of the servants of God," Bishop at Rome (590-604), had some pertinent words on this matter. The Patriarch John IV of Constantinople had claimed the title of Universal Bishop, and Gregory was prompted to declare that such a title was "blasphemous, antichristian, and diabolical, by whomsoever assumed."[9] Cyriacus, the successor of John IV, refused to relinquish the title. However, Pope Boniface III (607) did prevail upon the Emperor Phocas to take the title of Ecumenical Bishop away from the Bishop of Constantinople, and confer it upon the Roman Bishop. Phocas' decision on this matter was probably for no greater reason than that his predecessor had taken a different position.

Edward Gibbon, in his illustrious history *The Decline and Fall of the Roman Empire*, painted a villainous portrait of Phocas. His succession to the throne took place in the midst

---

8. Even if one would accept the view that Peter is the rock, the "Petrine theory" is surely still open to serious doubt. To what extent was Peter the leader of the apostles? (See *Acts* 15; *Galatians* 2.) Does the text really say that Peter was to have supreme authority, both legislative and judicial, over the whole church? Does it declare that this supposed authority is transmissible? Where?

9. Samuel G. Green, *A Handbook of Church History*, 1904, 344.

of great civil and military unrest. He was an obscure centurion but, once holding the reins of power, he soon manifested tyrannical cruelty. The five sons of the Emperor Maurice were murdered before their parents' eyes. Then the Emperor himself was put to death. The bodies were cast into the sea and their heads were displayed at Constantinople till signs of putrefaction made disposal necessary. Shortly afterward, Phocas completed the massacre of the Imperial family. The eldest son, Theodosius, who had been sent to solicit help of the Persian monarch, was apprehended and beheaded at Nice. The mother and the three daughters were executed at Chalcedon. Notwithstanding the monstrous depravity of Phocas, Pope Gregory not only acquiesced to the government of the usurper, but also applauded his accession with base adulation, going so far as to call it "a glorious work of God."[10]

Even with the aid of the notorious Phocas, the question of a single Bishop possessing authority and jurisdiction over the whole church was by no means settled. The controversy eventually led to the rupture of Christendom in the ninth century. Papal supremacy came to be recognized only in the Western half of the Empire. There had been ecumenical councils during the first five centuries; there were the many ponderous volumes of the church fathers; but there is no mention made of the doctrine of a Roman Bishop reigning as sovereign monarch over all the people of God. Such a doctrine was apparently unknown during these early centuries. When compared with the papal claims of the eleventh, twelfth, and thirteenth centuries, this fact is somewhat difficult to explain. Is it possible that so momentous a doctrine could have been

10. Augustus Neander, *General History of the Christian Religion and Church*, translated by Joseph Torrey, 10 volumes, 1851; Volume V, 156.

taken for granted? The answer could hardly be yes in the light of the controversy between East and West, and in view of the nature of later extravagant papal claims. How then did this doctrine gain such a solid footing in the Western half of Christendom?

Surely, no one would want to argue that the great historical differences in the extent and power of the Roman See between the sixth and twelfth centuries can be explained solely by reference to the words of *Matthew* 16:18. Popes such as Gregory VII (1073-1085), Innocent III (1198-1216) and Boniface VIII (1294-1303) did, of course, appeal to Biblical passages, but the actual exercise of their power can scarcely find valid explanation by reference to such passages. Of necessity, a more acceptable explanation must be sought somewhere in the milieu of historical forces and events which bridge the period. Such recourse can hardly be judged unreasonable. Little can be done for those who ascribe everything to the direct intervention of God, and who dismiss all discussion of intermediate causes. Such a mentality would make the study of history a complete waste of time. Yet, in certain ways, the Roman Church is almost forced into a conclusion of this sort with regard to history, because from the perspective of later doctrinal developments historical judgments could summarily be invalidated solely on the basis of ecclesiastical authority.[11]

The Roman Church and the Roman Empire

The relationship between the Roman Church and history poses some interesting problems. As has just been suggested, such doctrines as the primacy and universal jurisdiction of

---

11. John Emerich Edward Dalberg-Acton, *The History of Freedom and Other Essays*, 1967, 515.

the Roman popes are not derived from explicit statements of Holy Scripture. The same might be said for the dogma of papal infallibility promulgated in 1870. Most modern Roman Catholic scholars will frankly admit this fact.[12] If, then, there is no single text or series of texts anywhere in the Bible to prove these doctrines, from whence did they come? Self-evidently they reflect a post-Biblical development, which, of course, means that they were introduced at a particular point in history to meet the needs of certain groups within the church. This does not imply that they have absolutely no connection with Scripture. In the words of one Roman Catholic scholar, they resulted from a discernible "trajectory" of Biblical images. With reference to the doctrine of infallibility, the trajectory was truly amazing, reaching all the way from the first to the nineteenth century. When it was promulgated, it was declared to be a doctrine, which belonged to "the ancient and constant faith of the church."[13] Here, then, is a problem of first magnitude, for as far as Scripture is concerned the doctrine was totally alien to the early church.

In the nineteenth century controversy concerning papal infallibility, there seemed to be no doubt that the dogma, once proclaimed, would greatly enhance the position and power of the pope. How anyone could possibly imagine the papacy being more exalted or more powerful than it was in the Middle Ages is difficult to conceive. Yet, nevertheless, there was a widespread opinion that it would constitute a sort of a dark Magna Carta of ecclesiastical absolutism. In some way or other it was viewed as being the other side of the coin of supreme jurisdiction.

12. Richard P. McBrien, *Catholicism,* 2 volumes, 1980; Volume II, 831, 832, 837.
13. Geddes MacGregor, *The Vatican Revolution,* 1958, 169.

However, the juxtaposition of the two concepts cannot signify anything less than the conquering of history by theology, for as far as historical judgments are concerned, infallibility and sovereignty are intrinsically incongruous. By definition, according to the first Vatican Council, infallible decrees are irreformable. The binding of a "sovereign" ruler by the irreformable acts of his predecessors is historically unthinkable. Furthermore, the same paragraph, which defines the infallibility of the Roman pontiff, states that in promulgating the dogma, the Council was "adhering to the tradition received from the beginning of the Christian faith...."[14] One might wonder how this can be, since the concept of the infallibility of the pope does not appear in the New Testament. It must lie somewhere along the "trajectory" of history, which means that historians must research a complex concatenation of historical circumstances in order to discover how the tradition was started in the first place. According to the work of Brian Tierney (*Origins of Papal Infallibility, 1150-1350*, 1972), the doctrine emerged in the years around 1300. Of course, it did not appear out of thin air. Papal power must have achieved such heights that a doctrinal claim of so great a consequence could be argued seriously. How then did such power come into existence? Obviously, the historical dimensions to the question cannot be avoided.

As has been noted, the first five centuries of Christianity knew little or nothing about an actual supreme rulership of the Roman pope over all churches. What then, from a historical point of view, could make such an unprecedented claim possible? One plausible answer has been suggested by a number of historians. It is that there seems to be a definite correlation between the power vacuum created by the demise of the

14. MacGregor, *The Vatican Revolution*, 179.

ancient Roman civilization and the growth and development of papal power at Rome. Francesco Guicciardini (1482-1540), in his classic history of the Italian Renaissance, was clearly of this opinion. He claimed that nobody denied "that the transfer of the imperial seat to Constantinople was the first origin of papal power."[15] As a result of the transfer, the Roman pontiffs were left free of Imperial control, and they themselves began to assume temporal power. Thomas Hobbes (1588-1679), in his *Leviathan*, described the papacy as, "no other than the ghost of the deceased *Roman Empire*, sitting crowned upon the grave thereof. For so did the papacy start up on a sudden out of the ruins of that heathen power."[16] Call it a historical accident, if there be such a thing, but clearly, in the time-space continuum of historical happenings, responsibilities of a more secular nature were thrust upon the Church. These may not have been desired by any of the Bishops of Rome, but the historical turn of events could hardly have been avoided. "In the West" there was "the gradual disintegration of all effective imperial authority," which "made possible the growth of a quite different tradition."[17] In the words of another writer, "The popes reluctantly took over the role of the Caesars."[18] In effect, "the church came to be the new incarnation of Roman unity."[19] The transition is not that difficult to understand, for the church was the only institution strong enough to provide necessary leadership.[20]

15. Francesco Guicciardini, *The History of Italy*, translated by Sidney Alexander, 1964, 143.

16. Francesco Guicciardini, *The History of Italy*, 143.

17. Thomas Hobbes, *Leviathan*, [1651] 1950, 614.

18. Brian Tierney, *The Crisis of Church and State*, 1964, 9.

19. Norman F. Cantor, *Medieval History, the Life and Death of a Civilization*, 1964, 18.

20. Roland H. Bainton, *Early and Medieval Christianity*, 1962, 52.

A further contributing factor, which eventually led to the growth and extension of papal power, was Emperor Constantine's acceptance of Christianity, and the problems this entailed. Christianity became the religion of the Empire. The Bishop of Rome had the prestige of association with the Imperial metropolis of the world. Before long, questions concerning the relationship between church and state elicited no small controversy. Both were looked upon as being ordained of God, and each was granted certain powers within its own respective jurisdiction. For example, Constantine assumed responsibility for the external administration of the Church and left the internal supervision to the Bishops. The division seemed reasonable, but with the passing of time theoretical boundaries became blurred and the Bishops began to pre-empt the advantage of the spiritual estate over the consciences of men. An illustration of how this was argued by the Bishops can be seen in the letter of Pope Gelasius (492-496) to Emperor Anastasius:

> There are indeed, most august Emperor, two powers by which this world is chiefly ruled: the sacred authority of the popes and the royal power. Of these the priestly power is much more important, because it has to render account for the kings of men themselves at the divine tribunal. For you know, our very clement son, that although you have the chief place in dignity over the human race, yet you must submit yourself faithfully to those who have charge of divine things and look to them for the means of your salvation.[21]

21. *Readings in Church History*, edited by Colman J. Barry, 2 volumes, 1960; Volume I, 147.

In theory, the basis for the later more exorbitant papal claims of authority over the temporal power was therefore present as early as the fifth century. The subsequent centuries tell a tale of the see-sawing action in the struggle for prominence between the two. What may have sounded acceptable in theory did not necessarily prove so in practice. In one voluminous work, which deals with this problem in great detail, attention is directed to what actually happened:

> The powers were co-ordinate, and, in their own spheres, independent of each other. But, as a matter of fact, circumstances were too strong for theory, and not only did the definition and delimitation of the boundaries of the province of each power prove a task of insuperable difficulty, but each power in turn found itself compelled to trench in some measure upon the province of the other.[22]

By the time of the later Middle Ages there could be little doubt which power was trenching the most. When compared with the earlier centuries, the extent of the later papal claims appear incredible. It was not simply a matter of the pope's jurisdiction being limited to the clergy and to spiritual matters, for that was generally conceded, but it was that "*omnes subsunt ei jure divine*" (everybody is subject to divine jurisdiction), "*parem non habet super terram*" (nor has he any equal on Earth).[23] Such claims recur repeatedly in canonistic writings, and as Walter Ullmann wrote, they

22. R. W. and A. J. Carlyle, *A History of Medieval Political Theory in the West*, 6 volumes; Volume 1, 284.

23. Walter Ullmann, *Medieval Papalism, the Political Theories of the Medieval Canonists*, 1949, 77.

"have to be taken literally: the idea of hyperbole was foreign to the canonists."[24]

According to Ullmann, the controversy "papacy versus empire" was analogically related to the ancient antagonism between mind and matter: "Just as the soul is superior to the body, in the same way the pope is superior to the emperor."[25] It was Plato who had taught that the spiritual was something divine and, therefore, the most valuable and the most distinctive of man's attributes. Relating this to the spiritual and temporal powers, the conclusion falls logically in favor of the spiritual being the more important. There were, then, philosophical, Biblical, and historical reasons for exalting the pope above the Emperor.[26] These reasons were carefully mustered and masterfully applied in the papal claims that emanated from the Roman See during the Middle Ages.

Fabricating History

Also, in order to bolster these claims, a number of remarkable forgeries came into existence. One of them, the *Donation of Constantine*, laid the foundation for the territorial claims of the papacy. In the *Donation*, the pope and the clergy were bequeathed the privileges that had belonged to the Emperor. The significance of the transaction is important, for it highlighted the claim that the temporal was inferior to the spiritual. It also provided a theoretical base to rest papal power upon human as well as divine law.[27] More will be said about such forgeries in dealing with the development of papal power. For the moment, let it be noted that such documents were apparently

24. Ullmann, *Medieval Papalism*, 77.
25. Ullmann, 81.
26. Ullmann, 176.
27. Ullmann, 108-109.

accepted quite readily by Gratian (*circa* 1140), the founder of the science of Canon Law. In citing from the popes of the first four centuries, he is reported to have taken 313 out of 324 quotations directly from these forgeries.[28] These forgeries may have been less vital in one respect than one might think. Certainly they were useful in propping up papal claims, but they were merely addenda to an idea that was already entrenched in the minds of papal supporters. Their usefulness lay elsewhere: in intimidating opponents and in convincing the undecided.

Further discussion of the question of the origins of papal power hardly seems necessary. What has been said is sufficient to form an intelligent appreciation of its theoretical and historical foundations. When it comes to the consideration of the development of papal power, there will, of course, be some overlapping, which will shed additional light on this chapter. Also, in the following chapters, the discussion will reach to the Vatican Councils of 1870 and 1963-1965. From all this, the reader will be able to apprehend whether or not there have been any significant changes in the Roman Catholic hierarchy as to the nature and extent of papal power. At this point, what might be helpful is a brief summarization of what has been stated with regard to origins. As mentioned at the beginning, the question of origins is not an easy matter in historical study. However, when we look at papal power from the perspective of the Middle Ages, there does seem to be a detectable combination of interdependent factors which account for its historical manifestation.

28. Hans Küng, *Infallible? An Enquiry*, translated by Erich Mosbacher, 1972, 95.

Conclusion

First of all, out of the circumstances surrounding the disintegration of the Western half of the Empire, the Roman Church emerged as the only structure strong enough to provide some degree of unity. It was not, therefore, unexpected that the Bishop of the largest city of the Empire should be thrust into a position of prominence. He had no rival to speak of in the West. His See was comparatively free of strife. He was also at various times called upon to mediate in theological disputes outside his own jurisdictional limits. Added to these considerations, his See had the traditional distinction of being associated, however weakly, with the illustrious name of the Apostle Peter, and this association, more than anything, tied to the doctrine of apostolic succession, became the theoretical cornerstone in the development of papal power throughout the Middle Ages. The historical circumstances of the first five centuries provided the soil in which a complex mixture of Biblical, philosophical, theological, and legal seeds took root. From these grew a nondescript plant that claimed to be quasi-divine in nature. In essence, in the words of J. B. Lightfoot, "the power of the Bishop of Rome was built upon the power of the Church of Rome. It was originally a primacy, not of the episcopate, but of the church."[29] The same thesis, slightly more elaborate, is repeated by Walter Ullmann:

> Because it was situated in the capital of the Roman Empire, the local *Roman* Church had a special pre-eminence and superior authority, and its agreement to any ecclesiastical or religious measure proposed was for this very reason held to be essential in the interests of the

29. J. B. Lightfoot, *The Apostolic Fathers*, 1890; part 1, 70.

Roman Empire. This position accorded to the Roman Church by the imperial government to no small extent fertilized the ground for the later juristic pre-eminence and primacy of the Roman Church.[30]

30. Walter Ullmann, *A Short History of the Papacy in the Middle Ages,* 1972, 9.

3

Development before
the Reformation

A T THE outset, there is once again the problem of origins. Where does one turn to find what might indisputably be considered the first historical manifestation of the exercise of papal power? Even the use of the title "Pope" did not belong exclusively to the Roman Bishop. E. Giles, in his *Documents Illustrating Papal Authority* A.D. 96-454, cited archaeological evidence for the earliest use of Papa for the Bishop of Rome as belonging to the beginning of the fourth century. He pointed out also that the Bishop of Carthage and the Bishop of Alexandria were both called "Pope" at least fifty years earlier.[1] Perhaps, as some church historians have suggested, the first glimmer of "papal" power is to be found in the letter of Clement, the third Bishop of Rome, to the church at Corinth (A.D. 95?).[2] However, such a conclusion can only be deduced by inference and is somewhat doubtful. Clement did not really assert jurisdictional authority; rather, the tenor of his letter was clearly that of spiritual concern for the feuding Christians at Corinth, and he rebuked them

1. E. Giles, *Documents Illustrating Papal Authority* A.D. 96-454, 1952, xvii.

2. The episcopate of Clement is not without difficulties. See *The Apostolic Fathers*, Part I, 151.

for their unruly behavior.[3] By analogy, this would be little different from any pastor writing to admonish Christian brethren in a church other than his own. Certainly it would not mean lordship over them.[4]

The First Five Centuries

In point of time, the next reference that is generally cited to prop up papal claims comes from Ignatius, Bishop of Antioch (111). In writing to the church at Rome, he wrote of "her that hath the presidency in the country of the region of the Romans...."[5] If anything, Ignatius' words, rather than proclaim the universal authority of the Bishop of Rome, do little more than circumscribe the limits of jurisdiction exercised by the church at Rome. A better case for papal supremacy can be made from the writings of Irenaeus (A.D. 130-200?). He wrote five books against the heresies of his day, and in his writings only one passage can be found relating to the question of the primacy of the Roman See. Speaking of the Roman church,

3. For the Roman Catholic view, see Thomas S. Dolan, *The See of Peter and the Voice of Antiquity*, 1908.

4. Cyril C. Richardson, in his introduction to Clement's *First Letter* makes a number of observations worth noting: (1) There is no evidence that Corinth applied to Rome for a judgment. (2) It was nothing extraordinary for leaders of one church to send a letter of advice and warning to another congregation. The apostolic practice set a precedent followed by Ignatius, Polycarp, Dionysius of Corinth, Serapion, and many others. (3) Each Christian community seems to have felt a sense of responsibility for the others. Local churches were not conceived as being totally isolated and autonomous units. (4) This document was written in the name of the congregation. (5) It is very far from a papal decree and makes no claim to superior authority. (6) Basing its admonitions on the authority of Scripture, it exercises persuasion to attain its objective (Cyril C. Richardson [translator and editor], *Early Christian Fathers*, 35).

5. J. B. Lightfoot, *The Apostolic Fathers*, 1889; Volume II, 558.

he exclaimed, "For unto this church which holds a leading position among the churches must needs resort every church – that is the faithful who are everywhere – inasmuch as the apostolic tradition is always preserved by the faithful who are everywhere."[6]

Here again, the subject matter and context of the passage scarcely present the idea of a supreme *Cathedra Petri*. On the contrary, Irenaeus associated the Roman church with both Peter and Paul, and said nothing to give Peter the pre-eminence. Clearly his main concern was to lay stress upon apostolic tradition. Admittedly this would have been an ideal opportunity to spell out the case for the Petrine theory, but he did not do so. The context makes plain that he was arguing that the Roman church was founded by Peter and Paul; therefore, the faithful resort to her. The fact that the Roman church held "a leading position among the churches" in no way meant that the Roman Bishop was head over all the churches. Later popes, conveniently dropping out Paul, nevertheless used the apostolic association to further their claims to absolute supremacy.

A further case, somewhat doubtful in point of authenticity, yet one that became a substantial foundation-stone in the building of papal pretensions, is made from the canons of the Council of Sardica (346). They were only applicable in the West and, even if genuine, they by no means recognized papal supremacy. What they granted was appellate jurisdiction to the See of Rome. Before this time no provision had been made for an appeal from a provincial synod for a Bishop who felt himself wronged. In similar vein, Emperor Valentinian enacted a law in 372 "empowering the Bishop of Rome

6. Dr. Kidd, *Documents Illustrative of the History of the Church*, Volume 1, No. 74, 124.

to examine and judge other Bishops, that religious disputes might not be decided by profane or secular judges."[7] It is not surprising, therefore, that the Bishops of Rome, armed with the prestige of "double apostolicity" and with the position of appellate authority, should become imbued with the belief that their authority was supreme over the whole church.

Pope Damasus applied the expression "the apostolic see" to the bishopric of Rome in 378. It is a totally un-Biblical conception. The powers of the apostles were extraordinary and incompatible with the limitations of a local see. How could any apostle, let alone Peter, be viewed within the confines of a local pastorate without neglecting his apostolic duties? Notwithstanding this question, the term was adopted without any apparent opposition. Augustine used it around 416. However, he did not use it to support the doctrine of papal supremacy. To quote him as having said, "*Roma locuta est, causa finita est*" (Rome has spoken, the case is ended) distorts the truth. Clearly, he viewed the pope's decision as being only one element in the combined witness of the Western Church.[8] But he did allow the equation of expressions between "Roman See" and "apostolic see." All that was now needed was for someone to join together "primacy" and "apostolic see." This was done by Boniface I in 422, and was given permanent fixation by Leo I (440-461). Leo reasoned that since Christ commissioned Peter, and since he alone was vicar of St. Peter, that same jurisdictional power given to Peter must be his also.

The extent to which Leo's claims were acknowledged remains a debatable point. By the fifth century, the Roman See held

7. John Schulte, *Roman Catholicism, Old and New, from the Standpoint of the Infallibility Doctrine*, 1876, 245.
8. C. F. Rogers, *Rome and the Early Church*, 17-19.

a high position of respect. As was pointed out, it had been granted an appellate status over other Bishops by Imperial law. Yet, the details concerning the exercise of this authority reveal some interesting facts. Take the case of Apriarius, for example. He was an African priest who had been deposed by his Bishop. He appealed to Pope Zosimus (417-418) and again to Pope Celestine (422-432). The appeals sparked controversy. This fact clearly implies that there was no general recognition of papal supremacy. But more than this, during the controversy something happened which singularly underscores the absence of total submission to the Roman Bishop. Citations from the canons of the Council of Nicea (325) made it apparent that jurisdictional authority was understood to be limited, not universal. Incidentally, as Ullmann pointed out, the Church of Rome did not play even a minor part in this great Council of Nicea, even though in later years it was given credit for the leadership of this Council.[9]

At the Council of Ephesus (431) a small papal legation of three representatives was present. There they expressed the opinion that Peter was the chief of the apostles, the veritable foundation-stone of the universal church, and that his successor was the pope in Rome. This declaration reappeared in countless papal documents from the fifth century to the Vatican Council in 1870. Yet despite these claims, the papal legation played a negligible role at the Council. Even at the Council of Chalcedon (451), where Pope Leo's position was given exalted recognition, there was also undeniable limitation of his jurisdictional authority. For one thing, it passed canons

---

9. Walter Ullmann, *A Short History of the Papacy in the Middle Ages*, 1972, 6.

that maintained the rights of synods to act independently of Rome. It also awarded equal rights and privileges to Constantinople such as the fathers had assigned to Rome. When the Roman legates heard of this decision they objected. They produced a version of the Canon of Nicaea, which claimed, "*Ecclesia Roman semper habuit principatum*" (The Roman Church has always had the headship). They were confronted with the Greek original, and the claim was repudiated. They were apparently unaware that the words had been added at Rome. With regard to the matter of papal legates from Rome, the twenty-ninth Council of Carthage (424) had objected, asking, "Was it held that the illumination of the Holy Spirit had been reserved for a single person [the pope], and denied to great assemblies of bishops?"[10]

In spite of such conciliar objections, it seems apparent that the foundational groundwork for the edifice of papal power was laid during the fifth century. Also at this time, mixed into the conceptual concrete of these foundations were some literary productions, which were nothing more than legends and forgeries. The first, which served to reinforce later papal claims to temporal power, was the *Legend of St. Silvester*, which appeared between 480 and 490. The intent of its unknown author was to highlight the role of Pope Silvester (314-336) in influencing Constantine to create a new capital of the Empire. The credit for raising Constantinople to its pre-eminent position therefore went to the papacy. In one scene, the writer depicted Constantine, without his Imperial symbols of office, lying prostrate before Silvester. After this act of contrition, Constantine was reinvested with his Emperor's emblems and soon

10. C. F. Rogers, *Rome and the Early Church*, 25.

48

thereafter moved his capital to Constantinople. There was, of course, not one scintilla of truth in the whole story yet, it held such sway that by the eighth century it was incorporated into the more influential forgery known as the *Donation of Constantine*. In this later document, Constantine, before departing to Constantinople, supposedly bestowed upon Silvester vast regions of land in the Western half of the Empire.

Before the fifth century ended, further fictitious undergirdings of papal power saw the light of day. They were conceived in the midst of a papal schism between two candidates for the papal chair. Interestingly, the two factions, acting independently of each other, held their elections on the same day and almost at the same time. Symmachus won the day over Laurentius – not because of amicable concessions, but because of the intervention of the Gothic King Theodoric who sided with Symmachus. The factional fighting gave rise to a number of forgeries, which specialized in the invention of synods. One of the Symmachan forgeries contained speeches made at an imaginary synod during the reign of Diocletian (284-305). Another described a synod headed by Pope Silvester in which Constantine also took part. The whole point of the so-called *Symmachan Apocrypha* was to weave together historical and fictional details so that they would fit into the contemporary events lending support to the papal claims of Symmachus. One example of the nature of this support comes from the imaginary council that was chaired by Silvester. It comes in the form of a decree, which stated, "Nobody can sit in judgment on the first (apostolic) see which distributes rightful justice to all. Neither the emperor nor the whole clergy nor kings nor people can judge the supreme judge."[11] The importance of these

---

11. Ullmann, *A Short History of the Papacy in the Middle Ages*, 39.

49

forgeries can be seen in that they were later incorporated into a number of collections of Canon Law, and thus became part of the official body of Roman Catholic law. They added to the mystique of prestige that made possible the more extravagant papal claims of the later Middle Ages.

It might be argued that even without the legends and forgeries, the prestige of the Roman Church would have continued to grow. Historical circumstances were all in its favor. It was only to be expected that the Bishop of the first city be considered the first Bishop in the Church. To be expected? Yes, perhaps to the Bishop of the first city, but as has been noted, not necessarily to all other Bishops. At Chalcedon it had been decreed that Constantinople should be equal to Rome in status. From the Eastern half of the Empire there was granted a kind of condescending see-sawing primacy of respect, but not of actual jurisdiction. The shift of political prominence from Rome to Constantinople had caused a commensurate shift in emphasis with regard to papal claims. No longer could there be any claim of primacy by way of association with the capital city. If political status determined ecclesiastical status, then Constantinople should have gained the ascendancy. The Roman answer to this threat was to shift the emphasis to claims based upon the Petrine theory. However, even in the face of this new emphasis, the Western ecclesiastics failed to grant undisputed jurisdictional primacy.

From chapter 2, it will be remembered that the controversy over which Bishop was the ecumenical Bishop was still going strong at the end of the sixth century. Notwithstanding this fact, the fifth century seems to be the time when a distinct regal-sacerdotal concept of papal power began to be formed. For example, this seems to be nascent in the letter Pope Gelasius wrote to Emperor Anastasius, which was also mentioned in chapter 2. The Gelasian theses implied a subtle monarchical-type conception: "The pope as successor of St. Peter has sole [authority] over the corporate body of Christians, amongst whom the emperor takes indeed a vital place, but one of an assistant nature...."[12] Not all popes in the fifth century shared Gelasius' viewpoint. If anything, his importance in the development of papal power comes more into focus in the later Middle Ages when propagandists used his theses to support greater papal pretensions. In these early centuries there was some ambivalence with regard to the relationship between temporal and spiritual authority. Certain popes favored a more conciliatory tone toward the East and others maintained the Gelasian hard line. Apparently, Pope Symmachus saw no inconsistency in writing intemperate letters to the Emperor, while appealing for help to the Arian King Theodoric. Undoubtedly, geographical distance was a factor, for barbarian kings ruled Italy, and the Emperor was far away. But as the next two centuries reveal, the Emperors did not allow distance or papal pretensions to offset their own claims to possess the greater authority.

The Church-State Ascendant

While the battle between papacy and Empire was destined to sway back and forth during these early centuries, there was never any real doubt as to which held the field. In 482, Emperor Zeno (474-491) drew up an Imperial edict, which became known by its formula of faith as the *Henotikon*. It was issued entirely on the Emperor's own authority, and it fixed the faith for the whole Empire. The Emperor viewed himself

12. Ullmann, *The Growth of Papal Government in the Middle Ages*, 1967, 28.

as the divinely appointed mouthpiece on Earth. There was a fusion of the sacred and the secular, which was in accordance with the tradition reaching back to Constantine (307-337), and even to the pagan Roman Emperors. This combination of sacred and secular power gave rise to what came to be called "Byzantine caesaropapism." During the reign of Justinian I (527-565) the Imperial theocracy reached a high peak. His granting of an exalted position to the papacy was really part of his plan to re-establish the Roman Empire. It did not stop him from deposing Pope Silverius (536-537), who died in a penal colony, nor from imprisoning Pope Vigilius (537-555) and forcibly appointing Pope Pelagius I (556-561) as successor. By Imperial decree Justinian fixed the legal procedure for papal elections.

Such matters did not, of course, halt the papal claims to be the successor of Peter, the foundation-stone of the universal church and the teacher and head of all orthodox Christians. But then neither did these claims prevent the continued harassment of the papacy by the Empire. Emperor Constans II (630-668) did not hesitate to bring Pope Martin I (649-655) to trial for charges of high treason. Martin I had been consecrated without Imperial approval. He was tried and sentenced to death by quartering. The sentence was not carried out, but he was banished to the outmost limits of the Empire, there to die of privation. The stalwart faith of Martin I might be cause for admiration, but the episode nevertheless illustrates that it was the Emperor who exercised supreme political and religious power over the Christian world of his day. However, this was by no means the last word in the struggle. In fact, as was already touched upon in chapter 2, the battle raged with even greater fury during the later Middle Ages.

Toward the latter half of the seventh century, the papacy

under Agatho (678-682) defiantly claimed magisterial primacy. At the Easter Synod in Rome the Emperor was told in unambiguous terms that the Roman Church was his mother, and that she had never erred. Incidentally, on this score, the Sixth General Council held a few months later in November 680 condemned Pope Honorius I (625-638) as a heretic for his views in the monothelitic controversy. The conflict continued between Pope Sergius I (687-701) and Emperor Justinian II (685-711). In 692, Justinian convoked a council without consulting or even inviting Pope Sergius I. He required the pope to sign the decrees of the council, and when the pope refused he threatened him with the same fate as Pope Martin I. Two of the pope's trusted advisers were arrested, but the execution of the Imperial warrant against the pope himself could not be carried out because of the anger of the Roman populace. The gulf between East and West was widening, and gradually, while there may have been little further ideological development, the papacy was beginning to extricate itself from the Imperial framework. The letters of Pope Gregory II (715-731) make it very plain that the papacy had not been cowed into abject submission. If anything, they espouse elements depicting claims of superiority: "We derive our power and authority from the prince of the apostles, Peter, and we could, if we wished, pronounce judgment upon you, but you have already pronounced judgment on yourself and on your counselors; and you and they may just as well remain accursed."[13]

It would be false to imagine that the papacy came out of the power struggle of these two centuries as an uncontested victor. But there is little doubt that the position of Bishop of Rome increased in power and stature. It was the pope, who

13. Ullmann, *The Growth of Papal Government in the Middle Ages,* 46.

on Christmas Day 800, conferred the title of Roman Emperor upon Charlemagne and solemnly crowned him at Rome. By implication, it was the Roman Church that created, through the pope, a Christian ruler who was to be the protector and defender of the Christian world. Consider also the coronation of Louis the Pious (814-840) by Pope Stephen V (816-817) at Rheims in 816. Read the prayer said by Stephen after the blessing of the crown: "O Christ, Ruler of the Empire of the world and Master of the ages, you have willed that Rome be the head of the earthly globe, grant our prayers."[14] At their first meeting it was Louis who prostrated himself three times before the pope. The coronations by the popes of Louis II in 850 and of Charles the Bald in 875 were in the same tradition and served to provide increased prestige to papal power. The latter was presented with the crown "through the privilege of the apostolic see."[15] It was during this period that three great influential forgeries saw the light of day. All three – the *Capitula Angilramni*, *Pseudo-Isidore*, and *Benedictus Levita* – attempt to give the papal prerogatives the support of antiquity.

In the ninth century Nicholas I (858-867) with all the ideological arguments of his predecessors, aided by *Pseudo-Isidore*, was able to state the case for the plenitude of papal power more forcefully and comprehensively than any of his predecessors. He had the added advantage of the fruitful cooperation of Anastasius, a great librarian and church historian. The learned scholar hailed Nicholas as the "vicar of God," the "pontiff of universal mankind," the "*unicus papa*" (one and only pope), and also the "doorkeeper of Heaven."[16] Adrian II (867-872)

14. Ullmann, *The Growth of Papal Government in the Middle Ages*, 145.

15. Ullmann, 161.

16. Ullmann, 192.

did not take second place to Nicholas in his views and in the exercise of the papal office. He functioned as the vicar of Peter and claimed to inherit all his power. He considered himself to be the supreme monarch within the *societas fidelium* (faithful society), that is, over the corpus of Christendom. The successor to Adrian was John VIII (872-882). For John, the Roman Church had supreme jurisdiction over all the nations of the world. Disobedience to his commands was the equivalent of disobedience to divine commands.[17] His main contribution to the theoretical development of views of papal power was that society formed one body corporate and politic, headed by the pope, and ruled through the instrumentality of the priesthood.

During the tenth century the papacy sank to depths of degradation unparalleled up to that time. Edward Gibbon accused Protestants of dwelling "with malicious pleasure" upon the scandals of the period.[18] His charge might be well founded, but the judgment appears to be lopsided. More to the point, if "antichrists" (Gibbon's word) were running the Curia, what then became of the Petrine theory and the doctrine of apostolic succession? Not only Protestant historians, but also others without a religious axe to grind have referred to this whole phase in papal history as the "pornocracy." Be this as it may, in the pursuit of tracing the development of papal power, it seems unnecessary to dwell, with or without "malicious pleasure," one moment longer on this period. Besides, notions of power could hardly be expected to undergo

17. Ullmann, *The Growth of Papal Government in the Middle Ages*, 220.

18. Edward Gibbon, *The History of the Decline and Fall of the Roman Empire*, Volume II, 406.

constructive development during such times. This is not the case, however, in the course of the following three centuries. Despite that period events resulted in even greater advances in the exercise of papal power.

The Church-State Triumphant

From the accession of Leo IX in 1049 to the death of Boniface VIII in 1303, the papacy exercised, as far as extent and duration were concerned, its greatest degree of supremacy over European society. The tenth century and the first half of the eleventh century had witnessed the increase of Imperial domination, which reached its climax under Emperor Henry III (1046-1056). He was perhaps the most powerful of the early medieval German king-emperors. It was he, with some show of election, who actually appointed Leo IX to the papal throne (1049). Nevertheless, under Leo, a reform movement received impetus that followed a more centralized direction. He presided personally at councils; he took an active part in deposing unworthy prelates, in stringently penalizing simony, in insisting upon clerical celibacy, and in attempting to prevent lay interference in clerical elections. His actions were destined to revive the perennial problem of the power struggle in papal-imperial relations. Shortly after his death, the Lateran Council of 1059 dictated the famous decree on papal elections. Henceforth, popes were to be chosen by the cardinal Bishops of Rome, their choice to be confirmed by the cardinal priests and deacons and acclaimed by the populace. Leo's example, and the determination to follow him, introduced a new chapter into papal history.

Among the associates brought to Rome by Leo was the monk Hildebrand, the future Gregory VII. There was no disagreement between them over the need for reform and the role of the pope in the affairs of Christendom. If anything, Gregory intensified the papal claims by his views of papal authority. The most outstanding example of such views is found in a series of aphorisms called the *Dictatus Papae*. Some doubt has been raised over the authorship of these statements, but more than likely they are from Gregory himself. The quotation is somewhat lengthy, but it is too noteworthy to run the risk of missing something by attempting a condensed summary:

- The Roman Church was founded by God alone.

- The Roman Bishop is properly called universal.

- He alone may depose Bishops and reinstate them.

- His legate, though of inferior grade, takes precedence in a council of all Bishops and may render a decision of deposition against them.

- He alone may use the insignia of Empire (on basis of *Donation of Constantine*).

- The pope is the only person whose feet are kissed by all princes.

- His title is unique in the world. [This is the first distinct assertion of the exclusive right of the Bishop of Rome to the title of Pope, once applied to all Bishops.]

- He may depose emperors.

- No council may be regarded as a general one without his consent.

- No book or chapter may be regarded as canonical without his authority.

- A decree of his may be annulled by no one; he alone may annul the decrees of all.

- He may be judged by no one.

- No one shall dare to condemn one who appeals to the papal see.

- The Roman Church has never erred, or ever, by the witness of Scripture, shall err to all eternity.

- He may not be considered Catholic who does not agree with the Roman Church.

- The pope may absolve the subjects of the unjust from their allegiance.[19]

With the enunciation of such clear-cut concepts of the papal prerogatives, it is not difficult to see how the pontificate of Gregory VII led the papacy toward the establishment of a more centralized ecclesiastical institution. There were introduced a number of practical measures which brought the structure of the Church more closely in line with the feudal organization of the states. Legates were used to keep the papacy in better contact with local affairs. Provincial allegiances were broken down by requiring metropolitans to come to Rome for the pallium in person. Bishops were beginning to take an oath of fealty to Rome. Such was Gregory's power and prestige at this time that he did not shrink from deposing Emperor Henry IV in 1076. What student of history has not heard of the humiliation of Henry at Canossa?

About one hundred years after Gregory VII, the papal throne was occupied by a man who must rank among the greatest of medieval popes, Innocent III (1198-1216). The work of Innocent embraced a greater degree of systematization of theocratic

19. Joseph H. Dahmus, *A History of Medieval Civilization*, 1964, 525-526.

doctrine associated with papal claims than had hitherto been seen. He was able to a very large extent to implement the claims to ultimate and universal authority, which in certain respects had been the ideals for his predecessors. It was during his time that the theory of the two swords took definite root in Western Christendom. Bernard of Clairvaux (1090-1153) expressed the theory as follows:

> The two swords belong to St. Peter. One, the spiritual sword, is in his hands; the other, the temporal sword, is at his command whenever it is necessary to draw it. Peter in fact was told, regarding the sword, which seemed the least appropriate to him, "Put thy sword back into its sheath" (*John* 18:11). It was not for him, therefore, to use it with his own hands.[20]

The theory of the two swords – the one temporal, the other spiritual – was based upon the *Gospel of Luke* 22:38: "And they said, Lord, behold here are two swords. And he said unto them, It is enough." According to Brian Tierney, "A whole inverted pyramid of political fantasy was erected on the basis of this one verse of Scripture."[21] Both swords were at the disposal and under the authority of the papacy. In the letter *Sicut Universitatis Conditor* (1198), Innocent clearly differentiates between the spiritual and secular powers, leaving no doubt that the spiritual is supreme. He uses the analogy of the Sun and the Moon: The former represented the pontifical authority and the latter the royal.[22] In the decretal

20. Wladimir D'Ormesson, *The Papacy*, 1959, 63-64.

21. Brian Tierney, *The Crisis of Church and State*, 1964, 8.

22. "Just as God, founder of the universe, has constituted two large luminaries in the firmament of heaven, a major one to dominate the day and a minor one to dominate the night, so he has established in the firma-

Venerabilem Fratrem (1202), the argument for the temporal power being subservient to the spiritual rests upon the claim that the very "right and power" of the Emperor comes from the Apostolic See. Innocent's assertion is historically rooted in the coronation of Charlemagne by the pope.[23] In one of his sermons on the meaning of pontifical consecration, Innocent declared, "I have obtained from Peter the mitre for

---

ment of the universal church, which is signified by the name of Heaven, two great dignities, a major one to preside, so to speak, over the days of the souls, and a minor one to preside over the nights of the bodies. They are the pontifical authority and the royal power. Thus, as the Moon receives its light from the Sun and for this very reason is minor both in quantity and in quality, in its size and in its effect, so the royal power derives from the pontifical authority the splendor of its dignity, the more of which is inherent in it, the less is the light with which it is adorned, whereas the more it is distant from its reach" (*Readings in Church History*, edited by Colman J. Barry, 2 volumes, 1960; Volume I, 438-439).

23. "Just as we – who owe justice to particular persons according to the service connected with the apostolic office – do not want our justice to be usurped by others, so we do not wish to vindicate to ourselves the rights of the princes. Wherefore we recognize, as we should, the right and power of those princes to whom it is known to pertain by right and ancient custom to elect a king who is subsequently to be promoted to the dignity of Emperor; and particularly so as this right and power has come to them from the apostolic see, which had transferred the Roman Empire from the Greeks to the Germans in the person of Charlemagne. But, on the other hand, the princes should recognize, and they actually do recognize, that the right and authority to examine the person elected as king – who is to be promoted to the office of Emperor – belongs to us, who anoint, consecrate, and crown him. For it is usually and generally observed that the examination of the person appertains to him to whom belongs the laying-on of hands. Consequently, if the princes not only by divided votes but even unanimously elected as king a sacrilegious or excommunicated man, a tyrant or an idiot, a heretic or a pagan, should we anoint, consecrate, and crown such a man? Certainly not!" (*Readings in Church History*, 437-438).

my priesthood and the crown for my royalty; he has made me vicar of him upon whose vesture is written, King of kings and Lord of lords...."[24] In theory, the hegemony of the Bishop of Rome knew no bounds. To him had been given not only "authority over all the churches" but also "of the whole world."[25] During the pontificate of Innocent III nearly every European ruler submitted to the power and authority of the Roman Church.

Such intimate and direct association between the secular and the spiritual concepts of power made any theoretical system of separation difficult to maintain. If in theory the pope, as supreme representative of the church, possessed the right of full power over both church and state, any limitation of papal authority would be extremely difficult to define. Innocent tried to do this in the decretal *Novit Ille* (1204), but whether he succeeded or not is highly debatable.[26] This decretal dealt particularly with the papal plenitude of power and was concerned with removing any charges that the papacy was intent on diminishing the jurisdiction or power of the royal prerogatives. Innocent carefully enunciated the divine origin of his office and clearly established the claim that there were no bounds to his ecclesiastical powers with respect to persons. The only limitation upon his supervision was that the matter in hand must be related to spiritual and moral questions. But was this a clear-cut restriction of papal power? If political activity could be conducted outside the framework of moral and spiritual matters, there would be no problem; but if judged necessary, the papacy could find some

24. C. S. M. Walker, *The Gathering Storm*, 1961, 164.
25. C. S. M. Walker, 163-164.
26. *Readings in Church History*, Volume I, 436-437.

legitimate spiritual justification for intervention in almost every public event. The one whose title was "Vicar of Jesus Christ and Successor of the Prince of the Apostles," who was "the representative of him to whom belong the Earth and all that it contains and all those who inhabit it," could hardly conceive of papal power as being anything less than "super-power" with ultimate authority over both the temporal and the spiritual affairs of mankind.[27]

In case the reader suspects hyperbole at this point, it would be well to quote at length from the Bull of Innocent IV (1243-1254), *Eger Cui Levia*:

> Whoever seeks to evade the authority of the Vicar of Christ...thereby impairs the authority of Christ Himself. The King of kings has established us on Earth as His universal representative and has conferred full power on us; by giving to the prince of the apostles and to us the power of binding and loosing on Earth not only all men whatsoever, but also all things whatsoever.... The power of temporal government cannot be exercised outside the Church, since there is no power constituted by God outside her.... They are lacking in perspicacity and incapable of investigating the origin of things who imagine that the apostolic see received from Constantine the sovereignty of the Empire, whereas it had it previously, as is known, by nature and potentially. Our Lord Jesus Christ, Son of God, true man and true God...constituted to the benefit of the holy see a monarchy not only pontifical but royal; he committed to the blessed Peter and his successors the reins of the Empire both earthly and celestial, as is indicated by the plurality of the keys. Vicar of Christ [the pope] has received the power to exercise his jurisdiction

27. Wladimir D'Ormesson, *The Papacy*, 62.

by the one over the Earth for temporal things, by the other in Heaven for spiritual things.[28]

Papal power then, by the middle of the thirteenth century, was theoretically without limitation. According to Innocent IV, it was sacrilegious even to question the plenitude of the papal power. When the pontificate of Boniface VIII was inaugurated in 1294, the papacy was at a high-water mark in its pretensions. Boniface attempted to perpetuate the traditional papal claims, but in his day new forces were beginning to appear on the horizon. Nationalism was one such force, and Boniface found himself in disastrous conflict with Philip IV, King of France. It would be beyond the scope of this study to enter into the many details of the conflict. What is relevant is found in the assertions of Boniface with respect to the extent of papal power. Using the figure of the two swords again and emphasizing the divine origin of his power, he declared that the temporal was subservient to the spiritual:

> We are taught by the words of the Gospel that in this Church and in its power there are two swords, a spiritual, to wit, and a temporal...both are in the power of the Church, namely the spiritual and material swords; the one indeed to be wielded for the Church, the other by the Church; the former by the priest, the latter by the hand of kings and knights, but at the will and sufferance of that priest. For it is necessary that one sword should be under another and that the temporal authority should be subjected to the spiritual.... Whoever, therefore, resists this power thus ordained by God, resists the ordination

28. Bernard Guillemain, *The Later Middle Ages*, translated by S. Taylor; Volume 77 of the *Twentieth Century Encyclopedia of Catholicism*, edited by Henri Daniel-Rops, 1959, 37-38.

of God.... Consequently, we declare, state, define, and pronounce that it is altogether necessary to salvation for every human creature to be subject to the Roman pontiff.[29]

So great was the power of Boniface that when he presented the crown to the German Emperor Albrecht, it was given under the acknowledgment that the Empire had been transferred from the Greeks to the Germans by the pope. When Boniface received the German envoys, he is reported to have been seated on a throne, with a crown upon his head and a sword in his hand, and to have exclaimed, "I, I am the Emperor!"[30] In the bull *Ausculta fili* (1301), Boniface in his complaints against Philip re-echoed the sentiments of Gregory VII and Innocent III:

> God has placed us, unworthy though we be, over kings and kingdoms in order that we shall root out, destroy, disperse, edify, and plant in His name and by His doctrine. Do not allow yourselves to think that you have no superior and that you are not subject to the head of the

29. *Readings in Church History*, Volume I, 466-467. The more important formula of *Unam Sanctam* has been summarized by Henri Daniel-Rops: "(1) There is only one Church, outside which there is no salvation. (2) The Church has only one Head, Christ, who has delegated His authority to His vicar, the successor of St. Peter. (3) The pope has two swords, one spiritual, the other temporal; the first is wielded by the church, *i.e.*, by the pope, for the good of souls; the second is entrusted to kings, who may not use it except in the higher interests of Christianity and under the pope's direction. (4) The temporal is subject to the spiritual, which may pass judgment upon it if it goes astray. Consequently, (5) No one can be saved unless he willingly submits to the pope" (Henri Daniel-Rops, *Cathedral and Crusade*, 1957, 570).

30. Alexander Clarence Flick, *The Decline of the Medieval Church*, 2 volumes, 1930; Volume 1, 17.

ecclesiastical hierarchy. Whoever thinks this is a madman; whoever supports him in this belief is a heretic.[31]

The Beginning of Troubles

But, as already was mentioned, times were changing, and in the fusillade of verbal exchanges between Philip and Boniface, the claims of supremacy were being tested in the practical affairs of both church and state. Philip went so far as to attempt a plot to seize Boniface at the papal palace in Anagni and compel him to resign or bring him before a general church council. The plot failed, and Boniface died shortly thereafter.

Compared with the three centuries before Boniface VIII, there can be little doubt that the following centuries, until the time of the Vatican Council in 1870, witnessed a slowing down in the theoretical exposition and the practical exercise of papal power. In the words of Alexander Flick, "The drama of Canossa had at length been followed by the drama of Anagni."[32] Boniface may have believed that "it is altogether necessary to salvation for every human creature to be subject to the Roman pontiff," but the King of France did not. During the fourteenth century, the popes became hardly more than puppets of the French kings. Even the papacy itself was moved to Avignon (1309-1378). Following the "Babylonian captivity," as it came to be called, with the return of the pope to Rome, there was the scandal of the "great schism" (1378-1417), when two and sometimes three rival popes claimed to be the rightful successor of Peter.

31. Flick, *The Decline of the Medieval Church*, I, 25.
32. Flick, I, 30.

The fifteenth century brought the challenge of the conciliar movement. Men like John Gerson, Chancellor of the University of Paris, held that a general council was representative of the whole church and was superior to the pope. The fathers at the Council of Constance had ordained in 1415 that, "This holy synod…has received immediately from Christ a power to which all persons, of whatever rank or dignity, not excepting the pope himself, are bound to submit in matters concerning the faith."[33] This was the age when scholars were imbibing the spirit of the Renaissance, and also were challenging the *status quo* with the cry: "*Ad fontes!*" (To the primary sources!) Obedience to such a cry entailed destructive potential for papal claims to power. However, the full explosive force of this new emphasis, especially with regard to the study of the primary documents of Holy Scripture, was not really felt until some one hundred years later. It was then, under the passionate zeal of Martin Luther, that the Reformation had its beginning. Moreover, it was primarily Luther's acceptance of the authority of Holy Scripture that prompted his eventual open revolt against papal power.

It could perhaps be argued that if conciliarism had won the day the Reformation would never have taken place, but in history there is no place for what might have been. Within one generation of the Council of Constance, papal claims were heard again as loud as ever. The primary objective at Constance was to end the "great schism." This could hardly be done without general acceptance of the overall authority of the Council. In point of fact, the Council declared that all who held any office in the Church, including the pope, were to be obedient to the Council under pain of punishment.

33. Geddes MacGregor, *The Vatican Revolution*, 1958, 40.

"The main point of conciliarism," as Walter Ullmann wrote, "was that power was not located in the papal monarch but in the church itself as represented by the general council."[34] In a sense, then, even the pope was to be a servant of the Council. While it can be said that the Council was successful in ending the schism, it by no means settled the question of where ultimate authority rested. On January 18, 1460, Pope Pius II (1458-1464) sounded the death- knell of conciliarism in the papal bull *Execrabilis*:

> A horrible abuse, unheard-of in earlier times, has sprung up in our period. Some men, imbued with a spirit of rebellion and moved not by a desire for sound decisions but rather by a desire to escape the punishment for sin, suppose that they can appeal from the pope, Vicar of Jesus Christ; from the pope, to whom in the person of the blessed Peter it was said, "Feed my sheep," and "Whatever you bind on Earth will be bound in Heaven" – from this pope to a future council.... [W]e condemn appeals of this kind, reject them as erroneous and abominable, and declare them to be completely null and void.... [W]e lay down that from now on, no one should dare, regardless of his pretext, to make such an appeal from our decisions...from any commands at all from us or our successors....

> But if anyone – regardless of his status, rank, order, or condition, even if he be distinguished by imperial, regal, or pontifical dignity – should violate this command when two months have expired from the day this bull has been published in the papal chancery, he by this fact alone incurs excommunication from which he

34. Ullmann, *A Short History of the Papacy in the Middle Ages*, 299.

cannot be absolved except through the pope and at the time of death.[35]

On August 21, 1461, Pius II used *Execrabilis* in a bull of deposition promulgated against Archbishop Diether von Isenburg of Mainz. Pius II was well aware that the German church, universities, and courts were by and large strong supporters of conciliarism. Such a bias remained fairly constant right up to the days of Luther. At the Diet of Worms in 1521, a group of German princes supported Luther in his appeal to a council, specifically mentioning Pius II as being out of order in his prohibitions against future councils. Pius II's conflict with Archbishop Diether brought the curialist and conciliarist forces out into the open. Diether had been refused the conferral of the archiepiscopal pallium until he did three things: (1) come to the pope in person for the confirmation; (2) give consent to a crusade tithe upon all income of the German church; and (3) promise never to seek a general council, or assemble the German Electors or suffragan Bishops without papal permission. Not being daunted, Diether continued to appeal to a future council. This brought about his excommunication.

During the dispute an important tract appeared in defense of the papal position. It was by Gabriel Biel (1425?-1495), a theologian of no mean reputation, and one with whom Luther was well acquainted, as the next chapter will show. Biel's tract is divided into two parts: the first containing nine theses, all of which argue dogmatically for the Petrine theory of papal power; and the second setting forth twelve propositions dealing

35. Heiko A. Oberman, Daniel E. Zerfoss, and William J. Courtenay, translators and editors, *Defensorium Obedientiae Apostolicae et Alia Documenta*, 1968, 225, 227.

with the deposition of Diether. In the first part, Biel's reasoning moves back and forth over the single theme of Peter and his successors ruling the Church. His purpose in associating Peter, the apostolic see, and the Roman Church is to argue for complete obedience to papal authority.[36] "How could Christ have provided sufficiently for his Church," Biel asked, "if He had not perpetuated in the Church the authority granted to Peter to rule it?"[37] A more startling claim in this connection is the contention of Biel that the doctrinal definitions of the Church "must be believed with the same reverence as though they were stated in Holy Scripture."[38]

Biel's defense of the papal prerogatives was apparently sent to Pius II and was approved by him.[39] There could have been little doubt that approval would be registered, for Pius II shared the same sentiments concerning papal authority. In an encyclical he issued in support of his own candidate for the archbishopric of Mainz he declared,

> Since all kings and rulers of Christendom are accustomed to lend obedience and reverence to the Roman pontiff as the pastor and head of the Christian religion, it is only fitting that they lend support and assistance freely to this pontiff…against thieves and robbers, even against the impudence of the wicked who, despising the keys of the Church and striving to enter the fold over the wall and not through the gate, usurp with force the rule of metropolitan churches against the will of the pontiff.[40]

36. *Defensorium*, 85-87.
37. *Defensorium*, 91.
38. *Defensorium*, 75.
39. *Defensorium*, 58.
40. *Defensorium*, 349-355.

This encyclical began with the Gregorian superscription from the "servant of the servants of God," and ended with a promise of eternal life to all who would help the apostolic see in its endeavor to overthrow Diether, and who would lend their support to the installation of the papal candidate. That Pius II could make such a promise was based upon the claim, as he himself stated in a later bull issued in 1463, that there was no salvation outside of "the one catholic and apostolic church." Also stated very dogmatically was the claim that there could be no approved council without papal authority. How Pius II would have solved the "great schism" defies explanation. For him, all power flowed from the head to the members. This of course was only "when there was an unquestioned Roman pontiff."[41] Since he was "unquestioned" pope, conciliarism was a moribund matter. One of his successors, Pope Sixtus IV (1471-1484), made so bold as to proclaim that, "The authority to will or not to will a council is fixed solely in the Roman pontiff."[42] In a war between Sixtus IV and Venice, the Venetians appealed to a general council. The appeal was posted on the doors of St. Peter's, Sant' Angelo, and the Pantheon in Rome. The pope responded on July 15, 1483 (the same year as Luther's birth), with *Qui monitis*, pronouncing the appeal to be null and void, sacrilegious and detestable, and excommunicated the Doge of Venice and his supporters.

Papal opposition to conciliarism continued unabated into the next century. In July 1509 (the month and year of Calvin's birth), Pope Julius II (1503-1513) promulgated *Suscepti regiminis*, in which he insisted that *Execrabilis* was of enduring validity; exclaiming also that anyone appealing to a future council

41. *Defensorium*, 357-365.
42. *Defensorium*, 5.

would be considered a schismatic. Luther's challenge was only one decade away. Papal attitudes were adamantly fixed. How could any change be expected? The impasse was illustrated by the bull *Exsurge Domine* issued on June 15, 1520. Pope Leo X (1513-1521) was aiming primarily at Luther, but in doing so he drew ammunition directly from *Execrabilis* and from *Suscepti regiminis.* He likened Luther to a wild boar that had entered the sacred vineyard of the Church. Whether the image came from Leo X's immediate setting, for at the time of the issuance of this bull he was at his lodge hunting wild boar, or from Holy Scripture (*Psalm* 80:13; *Acts* 8:3) is a moot question. Leo X listed forty-one of Luther's supposed errors. Numbers twenty-five to twenty-nine dealt with the attack upon papal claims. According to inside information, which Luther received in October 1519 from a former fellow-student, Crotus Rubianus, then in Italy, the thing that angered the papal court more than anything else about Luther was his appeal for a general council.[43] Such appeals were viewed as open attacks upon papal power. However, the capstone in Luther's revolt took place at 9 a.m. on December 10, 1520. On this morning, Luther dramatically flung *Exsurge Domine* on a fire already burning with volumes of the Canon Law, the papal decretals, and Scholastic philosophy. The action was the climax of a three-year struggle, which had begun with the indulgence controversy back in 1517. It was a symbolical act that had momentous consequences as far as the future extent of papal power was concerned, and even the future course of European history. This study could hardly be complete without giving some consideration to what it was that brought about Luther's revolt.

43. James Atkinson, *The Trial of Luther*, 1971, 80.

4

Luther's Revolt against Papal Power

Luther's affixing of the *Ninety-Five Theses* near the entrance of the Castle Church at Wittenberg on October 31, 1517, was not in itself intended as an attack upon papal authority. In reality, as one author has pointed out, the event "had no more significance for his contemporaries than the positing of a subject for discussion by the Oxford Union would have today."[1] However, even though Luther did not consider his action as being indicative of disloyalty to any of his ecclesiastical superiors, it did thrust him into the limelight of public controversy, which, in turn, led to his open revolt against the papal institution.

Luther's First Intentions

Throughout 1518, there was no apparent indication that Luther had any avowed intention of formally breaking with the Roman Church. His testimony before Cardinal Cajetan, the papal legate to the Diet at Augsburg in October, bore this out. His words were as follows: "Above all, I, brother Martin Luther, Augustinian, declare publicly that I cherish and follow the holy Roman Church in all my words and actions – present, past, and future."[2] He was able to make

1. Trevor Gervase Jalland, *The Church and the Papacy*, 1944, 436.
2. Jaroslav Pelikan and Helmut T. Lehmann, editors. *Luther's Works*, 55 volumes, 1955; XXXI, 263.

this declaration even though certain doubts were beginning to arise concerning the papal system and the extent of its authority over the life and doctrine of the church. These doubts were briefly mentioned in his *Explanations of the Ninety-Five Theses* published the month prior to his hearing at Augsburg. But even this must not be interpreted to mean that he was consciously beginning an attack on the pope or on the papal office. In October 1518 he spoke of the pope as "the Most Holy Lord our Pope...."[3] A few months later, in January 1519, he wrote a letter to the pope and addressed him as "Your Holiness and August Majesty."[4] In this same letter he wrote, "I was deeply grieved that my most loyal service has had such an unhappy outcome and that what I had undertaken – to guard the honor of the Roman Church – had resulted in disgrace and was suspected of all wickedness, even so far as the head of the Church was concerned."[5]

In spite of the fact that he had already met with official ecclesiastical opposition in 1518, both at Heidelberg in May and at Augsburg in October, Luther still considered himself to be completely orthodox. The contrast, however, between what he said at the beginning of 1519 and what he said by the end of 1520 about the papacy and the Roman Church is truly amazing. By the middle of 1520, he was able without any mitigation to identify the papacy with the Antichrist of Holy Scripture and to declare without any reservation that the true church of God had nothing whatever to do with it. What brought about the change? In the preface of his *Lectures on Galatians*, published shortly after the Leipzig Disputation, he traced the beginning

3. *Luther's Works*, XLVIII, 89.
4. *Luther's Works*, XLVIII, 100.
5. *Luther's Works*, XLVIII, 101.

of the turning point to the days when he "babbled forth some trifling observations about indulgences."[6]

The Unintended Consequences

The intention of Luther in posting the *Ninety-Five Theses* and the unintended consequences of his action must therefore be distinguished. His primary intention was born "out of love and zeal for truth and the desire to bring it to light."[7] He seemed to be possessed of a naive confidence that led him to believe that all he needed to do was to turn the light of truth on and the darkness of error would vanish of its own accord. His opposition was directed toward what he termed "impious, false, and heretical"[8] teachings, which were associated with the granting of indulgences.

Luther, besides being a professor at Wittenberg, was a pastor, and part of the motivation for his becoming involved in the indulgence controversy came from deep pastoral concern. He wanted to see truth prevail, not merely to satisfy some intellectual ambition, but more directly because he believed that the propagation of error had eternal consequences for his flock. Luther's position on these points could hardly be intended as a direct attack on the authority of the papacy. If his contemporaries had understood it as such, Erasmus would hardly have declared that Luther's views were approved by the best men, and that the *Ninety-Five Theses* had received a universal welcome.

In spite of Luther's immediate intentions in writing the *Ninety-Five Theses*, within approximately three years of their

6. *Luther's Works*, XXVII, 153.
7. *Luther's Works*, XXXI, 25.
8. *Luther's Works*, XLVIII, 68.

publication his formal break with the Roman Catholic Church was a fact. His own testimony, as far as what prompted him to challenge the misuse of indulgences, was his emphasis upon the authority of Holy Scripture. He wrote that he was "measuring sins and errors by the standard of God's commandments and the most holy Gospel of Christ."[9] This point was of fundamental importance, for while some modern Roman Catholic scholars recognize that the particular indulgence in question "was being misused by the Curia and the Archbishop of Mainz"[10] and was a "classic example of scandal,"[11] it obviously involved much more for Luther. Consider, for example, what he wrote in *Theses* 32 and 62:

> 32. Those who believe that they can be certain of their salvation because they have indulgence letters will be eternally damned, together with their teachers.

> 62. The true treasure of the church is the most holy Gospel of the glory and grace of God.[12]

Even a cursory reading of the *Theses* reveals that the main issue was not primarily a matter of financial exploitation. Very clearly, Luther was concerned over the doctrinal aberrations that he believed were present in the instructions and the sermons associated with the sale of the indulgence letters. He felt that they were the cause of much gross misunderstanding among the people. For example, the Dominican John Tetzel, one of the preachers entrusted with the promotion of the

9. *Luther's Works*, XXVII, 153.

10. Christopher Henry Dawson, *The Dividing of Christendom*, 1965, 79, 80.

11. Philip Hughes, *A History of the Church*, 3 volumes, 1947; Volume III, 488.

12. *Luther's Works*, XXXI, 28, 31.

indulgences, purportedly preached that through confession, penance, and the placing of "alms into the coffer," a plenary indulgence could be obtained which could apply both to the "complete remission" of all sins and to the redemption of dead parents and others who suffer in purgatory.[13] A contemporary chronicler wrote that Tetzel claimed "that even if someone had slept with Christ's dear mother, the pope had power in Heaven and on Earth to forgive as long as money was put into the indulgence coffer."[14] Luther, in *Thesis 75*, appeared to support this report. However, Tetzel denied having made such a claim.

In a letter written to the Archbishop of Mainz on the same day that he posted the *Ninety-Five Theses*, Luther wrote more specifically about the confusion caused by the sale of indulgences. He manifested much concern about the false assurance of salvation that accompanied the buying of indulgences. He also challenged the teaching "that souls escape from purgatory as soon as they have placed a contribution in the chest."[15] In a more sweeping statement he declared, "Indulgences contribute absolutely nothing to the salvation and holiness of souls...."[16] In his estimation, "The first and only duty of the bishops...is to see that the people learn the Gospel and the love of Christ."[17] His reason for so bold a statement was found in the fact that Christ never "ordered that indulgences should be preached, but he forcefully commanded the Gospel to be preached."[18]

13. Hans J. Hillerbrand, *The Reformation*, 1964, 41-43.
14. Hillerbrand, 43.
15. *Luther's Works*, XLVIII, 46.
16. *Luther's Works*, XLVIII, 47.
17. *Luther's Works*, XLVIII, 47.
18. *Luther's Works*, XLVIII, 47.

Things began to move very rapidly after the *Ninety-Five Theses* obtained a wide circulation. The invention of the printing press proved fateful. Apparently, Luther's original intention was to keep the *Theses* for scholarly consideration alone, but to his consternation they were translated into German and made available to a wider audience. On March 5, 1518, he wrote, "I merely intended to submit them to a few learned men for examination, and if they approved of them, to suppress them."[19] Reactions to the *Theses* were somewhat contradictory. On the surface there was nothing in them that appeared revolutionary. Men like Sylvester Prierias (1456?-1523), a Dominican theologian and adviser to Pope Leo X, were able to study them and to conclude that Luther was guilty of heresy; while other men, like Cardinal Cajetan (1469-1534), the general of the Dominican order and a man reputed to have been "the greatest theologian of his time,"[20] concluded that they furnished no substantial ground for a charge of heresy. The problem, therefore, was not so much in what Luther actually said, but in what his statements implied.

Within a matter of weeks the *Theses* were circulated throughout the whole of Germany.[21] They had an adverse effect upon the indulgence traffic. Tetzel retaliated by attacking Luther, calling him a heretic, and boasting that within three weeks Luther would be in flames. The controversy was quick to elicit the attention of other theologians. In January 1518, Johann Eck (1486-1543), Professor of Theology at the University of Ingolstadt in Bavaria, published his *Obelisks*,[22] in which he as-

19. Albert Hyma, *New Light on Martin Luther*, 1958, 80.
20. Hubert Jedin, *A History of the Council of Trent*, translated by Ernest Graf, 1957, Volume I, 114, 158, 171.
21. *Luther's Works*, XLI, 234.
22. The word means "dagger points" and it comes from Origen's use

serted that Luther's views were similar to those of Jan Hus, who had been burned as a heretic in 1415. By this time the papacy had been informed of the disturbance in Germany. At first, Pope Leo X interpreted the trouble as a monkish quarrel, and did not take the matter seriously. However, in February 1518, Leo X directed the pro-magistrate of the Augustinian order, Gabriel della Volta, to send instructions to Staupitz "to quiet the man." The matter was brought before the general chapter of the Order held at Heidelberg during April and May. There appears to be little specific information as to what official action was taken against Luther.

During these early months of 1518 it already seemed apparent to some observers that inherent in Luther's views were some implications that challenged the power of the papacy. When the Archbishop of Mainz received Luther's *Theses*, he turned to the theological faculty of the University of Mainz for their expert opinion. After careful examination, they decided to put the whole matter before the authority of the Roman Curia. Among other things, they noted that the *Theses* limited "the power of the pope and the apostolic see...."[23] Luther had written to the Bishop of Brandenburg a letter similar to the one received by the Archbishop of Mainz. The answer, probably written on February 13, 1518, clearly pointed out that Luther was attacking the authority of the Church.[24] Johann Eck was of the same opinion. Luther knew this, for in a letter he wrote on March 24, 1518, he said, "In his *Obelisks*, he [Eck] calls me a fanatic Hussite, heretical, seditious, insolent, and

---

of such signs to denote questionable statements in contemporary literature.

23. E. G. Schwiebert, *Luther and His Times*, 1950, 322.
24. *Luther's Works*, XLI, 234.

rash, not to speak of such slight abuse as that I am dreaming, clumsy, unlearned, and that I despise the pope."[25] There were others outside the Church who also detected a note of rebellion against papal power. On April 3, 1518, Ulrich von Hutten (1488-1523) wrote to a friend, "Maybe you have not heard. A faction at Wittenberg in Saxony has risen in insurrection against the sovereign pontiff: Another is assuming the defense of the papal indulgences."[26]

As far as the indulgence controversy itself was concerned, Luther's interpretation of the "treasury of the church" was modified by an evangelical emphasis he drew from Holy Scripture. It was this emphasis that led him to conclude, "The saints have no superabundant merits…,"[27] and "The merits of Christ are, so to speak, a treasury, not of the Church, but of God the Father, for through His efficacious intercession before God Christ obtained for us remission of guilt."[28] These sentiments possessed, as far as Luther's opponents were concerned, some disturbing eccliesiological implications. By reinterpreting the doctrine of the treasury in the light of Holy Scripture, he dissociated the question of the doctrine of salvation from the framework of the authority of the Roman ecclesiastical institution.

Luther's Opponents

Luther's opponents seemed to have apprehended the seriousness of this matter before Luther did himself. Sylvester Prierias, the one commissioned by Pope Leo X to refute Luther, brought the issue into sharp focus when he asserted,

25. Schwiebert, *Luther and His Times*, 334.
26. Lucien Febvre, *Martin Luther: A Destiny*, 1929, 140.
27. *Luther's Works*, XXXI, 215.
28. *Luther's Works*, XXXI, 225.

The universal church is virtually the Roman Church, which consists representatively in the cardinals, but virtually in the pope. Just as the universal church cannot err on faith and morals, nor can a true council, neither can the Roman Church nor the pope when speaking in his official capacity. Whoever does not accept the doctrine of the Roman Church and of the Roman Pontiff, as the infallible rule of faith, from which the sacred Scripture derives strength and authority, is a heretic. And he who declares that in the matter of indulgences the Roman Church cannot do what it actually does is a heretic.[29]

During the Diet at Augsburg in the fall of 1518, the question of authority began to assume a more prominent place in the controversy. In August Luther had received a citation to come to Rome within sixty days to answer the accusations of heresy. Through the influence of his ruler, Frederick the Wise, this summons was changed, and Luther was to be examined before Cardinal Cajetan at Augsburg. The encounter took place in October, but it proved fruitless. Luther's account of the meeting appeared on November 25 under the title *Proceedings at Augsburg.* According to Luther, the difference between himself and Cajetan was evident. Like Prierias, Cajetan rested his case on the authority of the pope. For Luther the authority was Holy Scripture. At the first meeting Luther was requested to recant. He replied by asking to be shown wherein he had erred. Two of his *Theses* were declared to be contrary to Catholic doctrine. The first was the fifty-eighth of the *Ninety-Five Theses*, which declared that "the treasures of the church" were not identical

---

29. Roland H. Bainton, *The Reformation of the Sixteenth Century*, 1952, 41. [The reader should note the explicit statement that Scripture "derives strength and authority" from the Roman Church and Roman Pontiff. –*Editor*]

with "the merits of Christ,"[30] and the second was a sentence in the seventh *Thesis* of the *Explanations*, which stated that it was not the sacrament of penance, but faith that justified a man.[31] The meaning of the word "treasure" in the bull *Unigenitus* was also a source of contention.

Luther did not hesitate to declare that *Unigenitus* was a document characterized by verbosity and stuffed with ignorance.[32] His main criticism was based primarily on the way *Unigenitus* "distorts the Holy Scriptures and audaciously twists the words into a meaning which they do not have in their context, in fact into a contrary meaning."[33] Luther declared that the one thing he sought in the hearing before Cajetan was "the true meaning of Scripture."[34] With such a canon to guide him, he found it possible to question the traditional papal interpretation of *Matthew* 16:18-19. His emphasis upon the authority of Scripture led him also to take issue with those teachers who "fix the church of Christ in time and place."[35] He went on to declare that one can be a Christian without being in submission to the pope. He traced the title of universal bishop, which belonged to the pope, back to the time of Gregory (590-604).[36] And he viewed the power of the pope, not so much as existing by special divine right, but in terms of *Romans* 13:1, that is, as one of the powers that be. In

---

30. Bainton, *The Reformation of the Sixteenth Century*, 30, 261.

31. Bainton, 261.

32. *Luther's Works*, XXXI, 262.

33. *Luther's Works*, XXXI, 262.

34. *Luther's Works*, XXXI, 278.

35. *Luther's Works*, XXXI, 281.

36. *Luther's Works*, XXXI, 281. Luther appears to have erroneously inferred that Gregory I was the first to have received the title of "Pope" as head of the entire church and that previous Bishops had not used the title.

other words, it was to be supported and honored in the same sense as the secular power.[37]

Immediately after the encounter at Augsburg, Cajetan sought from Rome a less ambiguous statement about indulgences. This prompted the composition of the papal bull *Cum Postquam* (November 9, 1518). The content of the bull carefully pointed out the primacy of both the Roman Church and the Roman pontiff. As the vicar of Jesus Christ on Earth, the pope had "the power of the keys, to which it belongs to open the kingdom of Heaven, by removing the obstacles in the faithful in Christ…."[38] By virtue of his apostolic authority, the pope could "concede indulgences from the superabundant merits of Christ and the saints to these same faithful of Christ…whether they be in this life or in purgatory…."[39] The indulgence of the Church was to be "held by all and be preached under punishment of excommunication, of a sentence [automatically] imposed (*latae sententiae*)."[40]

The contents of *Cum Postquam* placed Luther on the horns of a dilemma. He had already made public his opinion that indulgences belonged to those things permitted by the Church. They were not meritorious and did not release souls from purgatory. He had been able to say these things because he believed the Church had not settled the question. What could he say now? *Cum Postquam* authoritatively and officially confirmed the arguments of Cajetan. What is more, the doctrine was binding under pain of excommunication. Luther viewed the "new decretal" as a most unusual document. For one thing, it

37. *Luther's Works*, XXXI, 239, 282.
38. Henry Denzinger, *Enchiridion Symbolorum, The Sources of Catholic Dogma*, translated by Roy J. Deferrari, 1957, 239.
39. Denzinger, 239.
40. Denzinger, 239.

contained no citations from the Holy Scriptures, Canon Law, or the church fathers. It was, therefore, in his eyes a collection of unsupported claims, which he could not acknowledge as being the doctrine of the "holy church."[41]

The early months of 1519 proved to be the watershed of Luther's career. Toward the end of January, Luther became entangled once again in controversy with theologian Johann Eck. On December 29, 1518, Eck had announced that there would be a disputation between himself and Karlstadt, Luther's colleague and Dean of the Theological Faculty at the University of Wittenberg. It had been agreed by the two theologians that the debate should be held at Leipzig. In preparation for the debate, Eck had published twelve theses he would defend. Eleven of them dealt with indulgences, and the twelfth concerned papal supremacy. The twelfth was clearly an attack on Luther's explanation of *Thesis 72*. Luther, in the *Explanations*, had raised some doubts about the jurisdiction of the Roman Church over other churches.[42] From what Luther read in Eck's theses, he believed that they were aimed at his own teachings. Therefore, Luther entered the fray and in February published twelve counter-theses. The last of these theses declared that it was doubtful whether the power and position of the pope could be justified histori-cally. It was evident that this was the main issue, and that the forthcoming disputation would feature Luther, rather than Karlstadt, as Eck's opponent.

Motivated by the renewed encounter with Eck, Luther was obliged to enter into a deeper study of church history and the papal decretals. On March 13 he wrote to Spalatin and

41. *Luther's Works*, XLVIII, 105.
42. *Luther's Works*, XXXI, 152.

made reference to his preparation for the Leipzig disputation. After describing the nature of his studies, he confided, "I do not know whether the pope is the Antichrist himself or whether he is his apostle, so miserable is Christ (that is, the truth) corrupted and crucified by the pope in the decretals."[43] During the course of the controversy, Eck added another thesis to the original twelve. It was concerned with the freedom of the will. This one became thesis 7, and the one on papal authority became thesis 13. Luther's response, his *Disputation and Defense of Brother Martin Luther against the Accusations of Dr. Johann Eck* was published in May. This work became the basis for the debate with Eck at Leipzig in July. At the center of the debate were the questions concerning the authority of the pope and the jurisdiction of the Roman Church. Luther's argument was that the primacy of the Bishop of Rome rested solely upon the papal decrees of the preceding four hundred years.[44] However, more than this, he clearly implied that the authority of the pope was contrary to the teaching of Scripture. He argued that Christ had not singled out Peter to bestow upon him alone a jurisdiction over the other apostles, which could be transferred to the successive Roman Bishops. He also asserted that both the papacy and church councils were liable to err.[45] Luther's position on the papacy was now out in the open and, so long as he held to it, there could be no hope of reconciliation with the Roman Church.

It was two months after Leipzig, on September 3, that Luther

43. *Luther's Works*, XLVIII, 114. The development of Luther's doctrine of the Antichrist is considered in John M. Headley, *Luther's View of Church History*, 1963, 181-223.

44. *Luther's Works*, XXXI, 318.

45. *Luther's Works*, XXXI, 321-322.

published his *Lectures on Galatians*. Not only did he repeat his conviction "that the council and the pope had erred and can err,"[46] but he apparently realized that his real battle was with the power of the pope and the privileges of the Roman Church. About this same time the implications of his emphasis upon the authority of Holy Scripture began to dawn more clearly upon his own thinking. After describing the theological confusion of his day and the lack of a common source of authority, he concluded that "Necessity itself compels us to flee for refuge to the most solid rock of divine Scripture and not to believe rashly any, whoever they may be, who speak, decide, or act contrary to its authority."[47]

The Empty Threat of Excommunication

He was not unaware that his views brought him under the threat of excommunication, and if pursued further would lead inexorably to excommunication itself. But, by the end of 1519, he had adopted such a concept of the nature of the church that excommunication was something no longer to be feared. The basic reason for this was that excommunication could exclude only from external membership in the ecclesiastical organization of the church. It could not really separate a man from the true church. To apprehend Luther's thinking on this matter, it is necessary to understand that he had by this time come to conceive of the true church as that "inner, spiritual and invisible fellowship of the heart, by which one is incorporated by true faith, hope, and love in the fellowship of Christ and of all the saints...."[48] This fellowship cannot be

---

46. *Luther's Works*, XXVII, 153, 158.
47. *Luther's Works*, XXVII, 156.
48. *Works of Martin Luther*, 6 volumes, 1915-32; Volume II, 10.

given or taken away by anyone, "be he bishop, pope, or angel, or any creature."[49]

In February 1520 Luther found occasion to read Hutten's edition of Valla's exposure of the *Donation of Constantine*, and as a result he wrote, "I have scarcely doubt that the pope is the Antichrist expected by the world, so closely do their acts, lives, sayings, and laws agree."[50] In the early part of June 1520, he added to this conclusion some words of exceptional vehemence which appear to mark a solemn and a final forging of his feelings toward Rome:

> Farewell, unhappy, hopeless, blasphemous Rome! The wrath of God is come upon you, as you deserve.... We have cared for Babylon, and she is not healed; let us leave her then, that she may be the habitation of dragons, spectres, and witches and, true to her name of Babel, an everlasting confusion, a new pantheon of wickedness.[51]

On June 15, 1520, Leo X signed the bull *Exsurge Domine*. Luther was given sixty days to recant or else suffer the consequences of excommunication. According to the relationship existing between church and state, excommunication would be accompanied by a ban under which Luther would be considered an outlaw. The bull began, "Arise, O Lord, and judge Thy cause...the cause of the holy Roman Church, the mother of all churches, and mistress of the faith...."[52] On October 10, or shortly before that date, the bull arrived in Wittenberg. It

49. *Works of Martin Luther*, II, 37.
50. Preserved Smith, *The Life and Letters of Martin Luther*, 1911, 73.
51. *Works of Martin Luther*, II, 58.
52. Henry Eyster Jacobs, *Martin Luther, The Hero of the Reformation, 1483-1546*, 1898, 413, 414.

was sent by Johann Eck, who had been largely responsible for its issuance. The senate of the university refused to put it into effect without having first received the advice and orders of the electoral court. Apparently the bull was not officially delivered to Luther personally. He had seen it and was aware of its contents, but it seems as though he decided to act as if it had not been legally turned over to him. On October 30 he wrote to Duke John Frederick, the son of Duke John, the brother and successor of Elector Frederick, "As the bull has in no way frightened me, I intend to preach, lecture, and write in spite of it."[53] Even as late as November 17 he appeared to have some doubts whether the bull would be put into effect. This may have been due to the fact that certain Bishops, like the one at Bamberg, refused or hesitated to publish and execute the bull in their dioceses. It may also have been due to the prevalence of the idea that final word on Luther's teaching could only be spoken by a general council.[54]

Exsurge Domine must have arrived in Luther's hands by December 10, for on that day (sixty days after the bull appeared in Wittenberg), along with volumes of the Canon Law, the papal decretals, and Scholastic philosophy, he cast it into the mounting flames of a fire which had been built expressly for such a purpose. This dramatic act of defiance was committed at the eastern gate near the Church of the Holy Cross in Wittenberg. Writing about it approximately one month later, Luther said, "I have burned the books of the pope and the bull, at first with trembling and praying; but now I am more pleased with this than with any other action of my life, for [these books] are worse than I had thought."[55] The papal bull

53. *Luther's Works*, XLVIII, 183.
54. Hubert Jedin, *A History of the Council of Trent*, 177.
55. *Luther's Works, A History of the Council of Trent*, XLVIII, 192.

had demanded the burning of Luther's books. At the instigation of Eck and the papal nuncio, Jerome Aleander, this had been done at Louvain, Cologne, and Mainz.

Before the year 1520 had run its course, Luther wrote the treatise, *Why the Books of the Pope and His Disciples Were Burned*. In this work he declared that the doctrine of the pope and his disciples was "antichristian, devilish doctrine."[56] He also, without reservation, identified the pope with the Antichrist of Holy Scripture.

In the early part of 1521 there could be no further question about the break with the Roman Church. Luther's excommunication was proclaimed on January 3, 1521, in the bull *Decet Romanum Pontificem*. But it was of no consequence to Luther, for by 1521 his attitude toward the papacy and the Roman Church had completely changed. In March 1521 he wrote,

> But I claim that if St. Peter himself were sitting in Rome today I would still deny that he is pope and supposed to rule over all other bishops by divine right. The papacy is a human invention of which God knows nothing. All churches are equal, and their unity does not depend on the sovereignty of this one man, but as St. Paul says in *Ephesians* 4, their unity depends on one faith, one baptism, one Lord Jesus Christ, and these are all in common and equal possession of all the parishes in the world.[57]

Scholastic Theology

Luther's revolt against papal power had led him to strike at the very heart of papal claims, that is, the Petrine theory

56. *Luther's Works*, XXXI, 348.
57. *Luther's Works*, XXXII, 82.

itself. The controversy had started inconspicuously as an inquiry into the power and efficacy of indulgences. But since the granting of indulgences was associated with the power and position of the pope, it was not long before this became the central issue. When Luther objected to abuses in the granting of indulgences, it was interpreted by his opponents as an indication of disloyalty to the pope and hence, therefore, to the Church. In Luther's own eyes this was not the case. He did not consider himself to be a traitor to the valid traditions of the church. But he was caught on the horns of a dilemma. The ecclesiastical authority with which he controverted claimed to be the visible embodiment of apostolic tradition. This left him with no alternative but to re-examine the doctrinal foundations of Roman Catholic ecclesiology.

In order to appreciate more fully the rationale behind Luther's opposition to the ecclesiastical authority of the Roman Church and his subsequent emphasis upon the spiritual nature of the Church, it would be helpful to gain a better understanding of the motives which prompted his concern over the scandalous traffic in indulgences. For Luther in 1517, the main question was clearly the false security engendered by the hawking of indulgences. At heart, it was a conflict involving two different systems of salvation.

According to the main traditions of the Roman Church, man was able to contribute in some way to his own salvation. This was accomplished by the accumulation of merit through the efficacious value of good works. In Scholastic theory there were two forms of merit. The first, known as congruent merit, was something which man received by his own application to spiritual concerns. By this process man received the internal grace, which then enabled him to perform works of a quality hitherto unattainable. These latter works were classified as condign merit, and they were the basis for more grace, and finally led to heavenly glory.

Luther, during his early years in the monastery, was caught up in a distinct stream of merit theology, which flowed from an academic-theological system known as nominalism. It had been controversial since the eleventh century, and by the fourteenth century had so pervaded the European universities that "nobody was allowed to ignore it."[58] An extreme form of nominalism, which was associated with the name of William of Ockham, had triumphed at the University of Erfurt.[59] This was the place where Luther earned his M.A. degree. One of Luther's teachers at Erfurt, Bartholomew Arnoldi von Usingen, was a dedicated disciple of Gabriel Biel (1425?-1495), who was one of the outstanding Ockhamists of the fifteenth century. Not only did Usingen stand close to Biel in time and thought, but he was "a true disciple of Biel with respect to the doctrine of justification."[60] There can be little doubt that Luther was familiar with Biel's theology. The textbook he read for ordination in 1507 was Biel's treatise on *The Canon of the Mass*. In October 1516 he wrote to John Lang mentioning that he was familiar with Biel, but that he disagreed with him on such matters as grace, charity, hope, faith, and virtue, adding, "He is a Pelagian."[61]

58. Etienne Gilson, *Reason and Revelation in the Middle Ages*, 1938, 87.

59. Ockhamism and "nominalism" are often used interchangeably, but according to Heiko A. Oberman, a noted authority in this field, "It is more correct to distinguish between them," the former being a more highly developed form of the latter (Heiko A. Oberman, "Some Notes on the Theology of Nominalism with Attention to its Relation to the Renaissance," *The Harvard Theological Review*, LIII [January 1960], 48).

60. Heiko A. Oberman, *The Harvest of Medieval Theology*, 1963, 180.

61. Albert Hyma, *Luther's Theological Development from Erfurt to Augsburg*, 1928, 40.

The significance of associating Luther with the theology of Biel emerges when one begins to understand Biel's doctrine of justification. First of all, it was theologically tied to ecclesiology. Biel could speak of "justification by grace alone," but only because he had made a distinction between the *potentia absoluta* and the *potentia ordinata* of God. The former signified the absolute power of God, subject only to the law of contradiction; and the latter referred to the order established by God in which he chose to act in providing man's salvation. Justification by grace came within the framework of *potentia absoluta.* Justification by works fell under the *potentia ordinata*, that is, under the divinely ordained jurisdiction of the ministry of the Church. In practice, it meant that justification was a process under the supervision of the Church. Man was to eschew evil and to choose good in order to create the proper disposition for the reception of grace. Unless man were able by his own power to do what lay within him, he could not merit the infusion of grace.[62]

There does not appear to be any substantial evidence to doubt that Luther was embroiled in this Ockhamist system of merit theology when he entered the monastery. By his own ability, aided by grace, he wanted to arrive at a pure love for God. He believed that if he did this, he could acquire the merit of congruence. If he thus provided the correct disposition, God in his mercy could reward him with his grace. Adorned with grace, he could then perform meritorious (condignly) works, by virtue of which he would become worthy to receive eternal life. With great earnestness he pursued this goal, but he could not overcome the torments of doubt and fear, the

62. Philip Watson has an excellent summary of these points in his work, *Let God Be God*, 1947, 15-16.

fruit of repeated self-examination, which revealed to him that he was falling short of the divine standard. He found that his very nature was infected by sin, which caused him relentless anxiety of soul. He was determined by strict observance of his monastic vows to find favor with God. Speaking of his monastic life, he said, "I was indeed a pious monk and kept the rules of my order so strictly that I can say: If ever a monk gained Heaven through monkery, it should have been I."[63]

The precise time and place when Luther resolved his spiritual problem concerning how God justifies the sinner appears to be an open question. Suggested dates range all the way from 1509 to 1519.[64] Luther himself, in his autobiographical preface to his Latin works written toward the end of his life in 1545, made it clear that he found the answer in Paul's *Epistle to the Romans*, chapter 1:17. However, this testimony does not allow for a definite dating of his new understanding of justification.[65] But there is good reason to suppose that he had arrived at his new appreciation of justification by at least 1516.[66] Certainly, by this year he had repudiated the Ockhamist doctrine of justification. In his lectures on *Romans*, completed in 1516, he declared,

> Wherefore it is mere madness for them to say that a man of his own powers is able to love God above all things and to do the works of the law in substance, if not literally, without grace. Fools! Theologians for swine!

63. Hans J. Hillerbrand, *The Reformation*, 1964, 24.

64. Preserved Smith, *The Life and Letters of Martin Luther*, 1911, 15.

65. Heiko A. Oberman, "*Iustitia Christi*, and *Iustitia Dei*, Luther and the Scholastic Doctrines of Justification," *Harvard Theological Review*, LIX (January 1966), 7.

66. Gordon Rupp, *The Righteousness of God*, 1953, 123.

According to them grace would not be necessary save for a new requirement above the law. For if the law is fulfilled by our own powers, as the way, then grace would not be necessary for the fulfillment of the law, but only for a new exaction beyond the law. Who can bear these sacrilegious opinions?[67]

Not only had Luther parted company with the Ockhamist theologians on this point, but he also clearly believed that he had arrived at a more accurate understanding of the divine processes of justification. On April 8, 1516, Luther wrote in a letter to George Spenlein, an Augustinian friar in the monastery at Wittenberg:

> Now I should like to know whether your soul, tired of its own righteousness, is learning to be revived by and to trust in the righteousness of Christ. For in our age the temptation to presumption besets many, especially those who try with all their might to be just and good without knowing the righteousness of God, which is most bountifully and freely given us in Christ. They try to do good of themselves in order that they might stand before God clothed in their own virtues and merits. But this is impossible.... Therefore, my dear friar, learn Christ and him crucified. Learn to praise him, and despairing of yourself, say, "Lord Jesus, you are my righteousness, just as I am your sin. You have taken upon yourself what is mine and have given to me what is yours. You have taken upon yourself what you were not and have given to me what I was not." ...For why was it necessary for him to die if we can obtain a good conscience by our own works and afflictions? Accordingly, you will find peace

67. Preserved Smith, *Life and Letters of Martin Luther*, 24.

only in him and only when you despair of yourself and your own works. Besides, you will learn from him that just as he has received you, so he has made your sins his own and has made his righteousness yours.[68]

With this brief background, it becomes easier to understand how Luther, motivated by a "zeal for the truth and the desire to bring it to light,"[69] felt that he was obligated to expose how vain it was "to trust in salvation by indulgence letters...."[70] By the end of 1517 Luther's theological thinking was increasingly becoming centered in "the most holy Gospel of the glory and grace of God."[71] He had given ample evidence in his lectures on *Romans* that he had parted company with the theology of human merit. Hence, before he ever stepped upon the public stage of history, there was implicit in his understanding of the doctrine of salvation certain principles, which, if carried to their logical conclusions, could serve to undermine the foundation of those claims that gave the Roman Church its peculiar authority.

Generally speaking, the medieval ecclesiastical system had made the Church an institution that was indispensable in the divine scheme of redemption. A doctrine of salvation by merit and an institutional doctrine of the Church were theologically inseparable. By mid-1518, Luther had come to believe that salvation was by grace through faith apart from meritorious works. By faith those who believed were made "one spirit and one body with Christ."[72] Faith, and faith alone, became the key

68. *Luther's Works*, XLVIII, 12, 13.
69. *Luther's Works*, XXXI, 25.
70. *Luther's Works*, XXXI, 30.
71. *Luther's Works*, XXXI, 31.
72. *Luther's Works*, XXXI, 190.

to participation in the benefits of Christ's righteousness. The sacraments were seen as "signs of grace," and were efficacious only when accompanied by faith.[73]

A Correct Understanding of the Church

There can be little doubt that Luther, by the end of 1518, was on the road to a concept of the church taking him further away from that held by his opponents.[74] It is difficult to say to what extent he was consciously engaged in developing a new formulation of the doctrine of the church, but he made it clear before the end of 1518 that he harbored no sympathy with the idea that the institution headed by the pope at Rome was the one and only true church. He referred to it as the "church," or more specifically as the "Roman Church," but he viewed it as one church among other churches.[75] It had become a "widow of Christ," that is, separated from Christ, and in need of reformation.[76]

The question of the position of the pope was more thoroughly dealt with in 1519 and 1520. By this time Luther rejected both the doctrine of the primacy and any claim of infallibility associated with the Roman See.[77] In the *Resolutiones Lutherianae super proposititionibus suis Lipsiae disputatis*, he left no questions about his attitude toward the authority of the pope. Papal power did not exist by divine right.[78] It was the result of history and custom. Whatever power the Roman Church might

73. *Luther's Works*, XXXI, 193.
74. This is evident both in the *Explanations of the Ninety-Five Theses*, and in the *Proceedings at Augsburg*.
75. *Luther's Works*, XXXI, 152.
76. *Luther's Works*, XXXI, 237, 250.
77. *Luther's Works*, XXXI, 152, 171.
78. *Martin Luthers Werke*, Volume II, 201.

possess by divine right, the same power was equally possessed by all other churches.[79] He contended that there was no divine basis for the distinction between priests, bishops, archbishops, patriarchs, or popes.[80] This also rested on history, custom, and law. The whole structure of the medieval ecclesiastical system was now without foundation. If the papacy did not exist by divine right, then it could not be above historical judgment.

From 1521 to 1541, a period of twenty years, Luther's gradual elaboration of the nature of the church did not depart from its essentially spiritual nature. The true church was a spiritual reality, visible only to men of faith. If the word "church" was used to describe an external structure or an ecclesiastical order that all men were able to perceive, it took on a different meaning. These two ideas were kept separate. Belonging to an external ecclesiastical group was no guarantee of membership of the true spiritual church. There was little variation in these sentiments even in the last years of his life.

In his last great treatise *Against the Roman Papacy, an Institution of the Devil* (1545) Luther dealt particularly with papal claims. It was divided into three parts: (1) the question of papal supremacy; (2) the right to judge and depose the popes; and (3) the claim that the pope brought the reign of the Roman Empire from the Greeks to the Germans.[81] This polemical treatise, perhaps the most bitter of Luther's writings, made it plain that he believed the papacy to be an institution founded by the devil.[82] It was not established by the temporal authority because that "does not have the power to do this in the kingdom

79. *Martin Luthers Werke*, II, 208.
80. *Martin Luthers Werke*, II, 432.
81. *Martin Luthers Werke*, II, 289-290.
82. *Martin Luthers Werks*, II, 296.

of God."[83] It was not the work of the spiritual powers, for the Bishops and councils had fought against it.[84] Because it did not come from the church, and it did not come from the temporal authority, Luther concluded that it came from the devil.[85] By a detailed analysis of many Scripture passages, especially of *Matthew* 16 and *John* 21:15, and by a consideration of historical events and papal decrees, Luther built his case against the papacy. In the conclusion to Part I, he wrote,

> We know that in Christendom it has been so arranged that all churches are equal, and there is only one single church of Christ in the world, as we pray, "I believe in one holy, Christian church." The reason is this: Wherever there is a church, anywhere in the whole world, it still has no other Gospel and Scripture, no other baptism and communion, no other faith and Spirit, no other Christ and God, no other Lord's Prayer and prayer, no other hope and eternal life than we have here in our church in Wittenberg. And their bishops are equal to our bishops, pastors, or preachers; none is lord or servant of the other; they all have the same kind and heart; and everything belonging to the church is equal.[86]

Overall, what Luther said in this treatise was principally an elaboration of what he had written in 1520-1521. The main difference was in the increased animosity toward the papacy. Luther called the papacy "my great anguish" (*meine grosse Anfechtung*). He was convinced that it could not be considered a neutral institution. If anything, it was Antichristian and

---

83. *Martin Luthers Werke*, II, 298.
84. *Martin Luthers Werke*, II, 299.
85. *Martin Luthers Werke*, II, 301.
86. *Martin Luthers Werke*, II, 358.

demonic. It was entangled in secular and political matters. It brought souls into fear and bondage with its legalism. It exalted the traditions of men above the Word of God.

In spite of everything Luther said about the papacy, he was willing to admit that there were true Christians in the Roman Church. This was simply because the Christian church and the Roman Church were not one and the same thing.[87] The treatise served to bring out the difference between them. According to Luther, the church remained primarily a spiritual entity. His emphasis was placed against the extravagant claims made by the supporters of the papal view of the church. Their claims made the church to be synonymous with the ecclesiastical institution headed by the pope.[88] Luther continued in his belief that the church was "the communion of saints." It was a "spiritual, living assembly" of people who had believed the Gospel and who owned Christ as their Sovereign.[89] The doctrine of the church he put forward in this treatise was essentially the same as that which appeared in his other Reformation writings. He closed the treatise with reference to his desire to write more on the subject of "devilish popery," but he died before this was accomplished.[90]

Luther's departure from papal thinking about the church remained firmly fixed throughout his whole Reformation career. To state it simply, he could not identify the papal institution with the true church of Christ, because it did not give heed to the Word of the Lord and did not teach true doctrine. "Heretofore," he declared, "the papacy alone wanted to be called the church…, but they are nothing else than the very opponents

87. *Martin Luthers Werke*, II, 296, 311.
88. *Martin Luthers Werke*, II, 293, 294.
89. *Martin Luthers Werke*, II, 308, 309.
90. *Martin Luthers Werke*, II, 376.

and enemies of Christ, the persecutors and destroyers of his kingdom."[91] The pope claimed to be the Vicar of Christ for the people of God because he supposedly sat in the seat of the Apostles Peter and Paul.[92] "Even a dog or a swine," exclaimed Luther, "can sit in the place of St. Peter."[93] The point here was not one of acerbity. Luther wanted it to be understood that just as a religious organization in itself did not constitute a true church, so historical continuity by itself could not be the sole distinction between the true and false church. Any taunt such as "Where was your church before Luther?" obviously fails to appreciate Luther's view of what constituted the true church.

Luther clearly perceived that there was a difference between the *ecclesia* of the New Testament and the institutionalized Roman Church. A great part of the Reformation controversy raged because of Luther's reaction against the *quid pro quo* that tried to identify them.[94] Theologians like Eck and Prierias were adamant in teaching that the church Christ established was coterminous with the institution headed by the pope. All the rights and privileges ascribed to the church of the New Testament were assigned to the papal institution. With this view Luther had no quarter. Yet it is clear that he saw historical continuity from the first-century Christian church until his day. In fact, he believed that the church dated back to Adam and Eve,[95] and that it would always exist on Earth "until the Last Day."[96] Even

---

91. *Luther's Works*, XIII, 286.
92. *Luther's Works*, IV, 348.
93. *Luther's Works*, IV, 348.
94. Jaroslav Pelikan, *Obedient Rebels*, 1964, 27.
95. *Luther's Works*, XIII, 90.
96. *Luther's Works*, XIII, 324.

throughout the darkness of the papal period God had preserved a remnant of his people.[97]

Luther believed the historical church had become alienated
from the church of the New Testament. He objected to Roman
Catholicism in the light of his Biblically-oriented theology. It
is important that this be understood, for the principle which
motivated Luther in his view of the church was "the determination to go back to and renew the original life of Christianity."[98] Luther realized that the institutional Church of his day
had developed by a long process of transformation out of the
original Christian society of the New Testament. The papacy
itself was a prime example of the entrance of human traditions
into the life of the church. Luther recognized this fact even
in the formative years of the Reformation. In his *Defense and
Explanation of All the Articles*, written in response to the bull
Exsurge Domine, he boldly asserted, "The papacy is a human
invention of which God knows nothing."[99] Certainly there was
nothing of it in Holy Scripture. As to its historical inception,
it dated back to about the time of Jerome.[100] These human
traditions, which Luther spoke of as "outward pretensions
and man-made laws," had been responsible for the origin and
development of all manner of "abominations and errors" in
the church.[101] But in spite of the doctrinal perversions of which
the Roman Church was guilty, Luther held that the true church
had perpetuated itself and was still present in his day, although
this could only be understood by faith in the Gospel.

97. *Works of Martin Luther*, V, 269.
98. Emil Brunner, *The Misunderstanding of the Church*, translated by
Harold Knight, 1952, 96.
99. *Luther's Works*, XXXII, 82.
100. *Luther's Works*, LI, 78.
101. *Luther's Works*, XXXII, 7.

Any attempt to undo the ecclesiastical traditions developed throughout history did not, in Luther's mind, contradict the historical continuity of the true church.[102] The church existed in his day, and it sustained a direct historical link with the New Testament apostles.[103] Believing this, he taught that there was no salvation outside the church, for in his own words: "Christ is to be found only where the Word is preached, and the Word is not preached except in the Christian church."[104] A sinner came to Christ only by means of the Gospel, which was proclaimed in the church. Luther was not teaching that membership in a church organization was the condition of salvation. To make him say this would be to misread. In his own words, he said, "Anyone who is to find Christ must first find the church…. Now the church is not wood and stone, but the company of people who believe in Christ…. Christ is certainly in their midst. Outside the Christian church there is no truth, no Christ, and no salvation."[105]

As far as the unity of the church was concerned, it was not a matter dependent upon maintaining the *status quo* of the ecclesiastical system. This would make it contingent upon human invention. Instead, Luther saw the unity of the church in connection with the Gospel of Christ.[106] He did not despise organizational and liturgical order, but such things did not make the church. As long as the Gospel was proclaimed through the spoken word and the sacraments, the church

102. Emil Brunner, *The Misunderstanding of the Church*, 97.

103. Geddes MacGregor, *Corpus Christi, The Nature of the Church According to the Reformed Tradition*, 1958, 8.

104. *Works of Martin Luther*, II, 373.

105. Lennart Pinomaa, *Faith Victorious*, translated by Walter J. Kukkonen, 1963, 117.

106. John M. Headley, *Luther's View of Church History*, 1963, 29.

continued. The Gospel might not be proclaimed altogether purely, but where it evoked faith, there existed the church. Ecclesiastical organizations may at times have obscured the light of the Gospel, as, for example, they did in his own day, but they could not destroy the church. What Luther wanted was simply to introduce an *instauratio catholica,* that is, "to lead the One Catholic Apostolic Church founded by Christ and endowed by him with ministry, Word, and Sacrament, back to its purely spiritual activity of proclaiming the Word which creates faith."[107]

The church, then, for Luther, was essentially a spiritual fellowship of believing souls who had been born again by the Holy Spirit through faith in the Gospel.[108] In this definition of the church the most commonly repeated terms were those that involved personal relationships rather than an impersonal organization. He saw the church as a "people," "God's people," "the community of believers," and the "*communio sanctorum.*" It existed on the Earth by the Word of God and by faith. Its uninterrupted continuity was not in the succession of Bishops, but in the succession of the faithful. He believed that this interpretation of the church was a recovery of the early Christian idea as revealed in the Holy Scriptures.

Luther's appeal to the authority of Holy Scripture is the master key to understanding his conflict with the hierarchy of the Roman Church. From this divinely inspired source he derived his concept of the church. As this became clear to his mind, he realized that he could not compromise with that view of the church that was bound to the exclusive preroga-

107. Ernst Troeltsch, *The Social Teaching of the Christian Churches,* translated by Olive Wyon, 2 volumes, 1956; Volume 2, 478.
108. *Luther's Works,* IV, 348-349.

tives of papal claims. Also, since these same claims supported the "hog-theologians," with their sacramental-merit theology, revolt was inevitable.

Here, in the final analysis, lay the basic cause of the Reformation. Essentially, it centered in theological controversy between two opposing systems of salvation, which could not be reconciled, since two incompatible criteria were vying with each other as sources of authority. The one was related inextricably to papal claims and the other was determined solely by appeal to Holy Scripture. It should be self-evident to any thinking person that there can be no hope of repairing the breach between Roman Catholicism and so-called traditional Protestantism while each continues to hold to its own distinctive court of authority. There is perhaps no theological question more important in this or in any age than that which lies behind the issue of authority. In this connection, Edward J. Carnell asked, "Do we find the truth by submitting to the church, or do we find the church by submitting to the truth?"[109] The Roman Church defends the first possibility, while those in the Reformation tradition defend the second.

Luther's own position was made very clear at the Diet of Worms in 1521. Thomas Carlyle called it the greatest moment in modern history. Before the Emperor himself, and the great ecclesiastical representatives of papal power, Luther was confronted by a collection of his books. He was asked to repudiate them, and to recant the errors they supposedly contained. He answered,

> Unless I am convicted by Scripture and plain reason
> (since I believe neither in the authority of popes and

109. Edward John Carnell, *The Case for Biblical Christianity*, edited by Ronald H. Nash, 1969, 26.

councils, for they have often erred and contradicted themselves), I am conquered by the Scriptures quoted by me, and my conscience is captive to the Word of God. I cannot and I will not recant anything, for to go against conscience is unsafe and dangerous. Here I stand, I can do no other. God help me. Amen.[110]

110. John C. L. Gieseler, *A Text-Book of Church History*, translated by Henry B. Smith, 5 volumes, 1876, Volume IV, 57. The Latin and the German from which the quotation was translated are as follows: *Nisi convictus fuero testimoniis Scripturarum, aut ratione evidente (nam neque Papae, neque Conciliis solis credo, cum constet eos errasse saepius, et sibi ipsis contradixisse); victus sum Scripturis a me adductis, captaque est conscientia in verbis Dei, revocare neque possum, neque volo quidquam, cum contra conscientiam agere neque tutum sit neque integrum. Hie stehe ich, ich kann nicht anders, Gott helf mir, Amen.*

5

Development after
the Reformation

T HE final page of Geoffrey Barraclough's book *The Medieval Papacy* contains this judgment: "The medieval papacy ended in bankruptcy." Furthermore, he pondered the possibility "whether but for Luther, it might not have carried medieval Christendom – or Western Christendom – into bankruptcy with it."[1]

Luther was by no means the first to call for a reformation of the church. Throughout the whole of the fifteenth century, and on into the sixteenth century, there was much discussion among thoughtful men concerning the need to reform the abuses within the Roman Church, and particularly within the Curia itself. Francesco Guicciardini (1483-1540) wrote, "So much evil cannot be said of the Roman Curia that more does not deserve to be said of it, for it is an infamy, an example of the shame and wickedness of the world."[2] Moreover, rather than put themselves at the head of such a movement of moral reformation, the popes appeared inclined, more often than not, to be actively involved in seeking to prevent it. Not only the popes, but the cardinals also, according to Guicciardini,

1. Geoffrey Barraclough, *The Medieval Papacy*, 1979, 196.
2. Quoted in Preserved Smith, *The Age of the Reformation*, 1930, 373.

were suspicious of the reforms a council might introduce.[3] Following the Reformation, the Emperor himself added his weight to insist on a council, but his assurances to protect papal interests fell on deaf ears. In the opinion of Hubert Jedin, who wrote the definitive hisory of the Council of Trent (1545-1563), this general antipathy toward a reforming council was a dreadful mistake.[4]

Ever since the days of Pius II and *Execrabilis*, papal opposition to the theory of reforming councils had become almost endemic. If anything, the Reformation had served to intensify the antagonism between curialist and conciliarist forces. Yet, at the same time, the hierarchy of the Roman Church was on the horns of a dilemma, for with Luther's victories and the widespread acceptance of his teachings, retrenchment was hardly an advisable course of action. More fitting would be a counter-offensive, if not a "Counter-Reformation." It was obviously a time for extraordinary measures if the spread of Protestantism was to be halted. How best then to offset the exigencies of what to Roman Catholic eyes was a serious threat to the very foundation of the Church?

The Counter-Reformation

The first serious attempt at some degree of reform was made by Leo X's non-Italian successor, Adrian VI (1522-1523). However, it was doomed to failure. First of all, Adrian VI's pontificate was too short. Second, he found the corruption at Rome to be invincible. Third, his prescribed medication

3. Francesco Guicciardini, *The History of Italy*, translated by Sidney Alexander, 1969, 433.

4. Hubert Jedin, *A History of the Council of Trent*, translated by Ernest Graf, 1957; Volume I, 137.

to help cure the illness was viewed as being worse than the disease itself. Rather than mourning, there was much relief at his passing. His successor, Clement VII (1523-1534), a descendent of the Florentine Medici, was a vacillating, pusillanimous individual who did little more than toy with the idea of a reforming council. When a rumor of such a council caused the prices of saleable ecclesiastical offices to dwindle, he quickly squelched the rumor. One of his contemporaries described his pontificate as being "one of scruples, considerations, and discords, of buts and ifs and thens and moreovers, and plenty of words without effect."[5] Of course, Clement VII was not alone in his aversion to a council. Aleander, a papal legate, advised him, "Never offer a council, never refuse it directly. On the contrary, show you are willing to comply with the request, but stress the difficulties in the way. Thus you will be able to ward it off."[6] The primary reason for papal opposition to reforming councils remained essentially the same. It was basically a fear of infringement of pontifical power. Why run the risk of reviving conciliarism?

Pressure for a reforming council continued to mount. Nationalism was on the rise. During Clement VII's reign, England repudiated papal authority and royal supremacy became an accomplished fact. The only countries remaining solidly in the papal camp were Italy and Spain. However, with the pontificate of Paul III (1534-1549), there was a noticeable turning point. No sooner was he elected than he announced that the work of reform would begin. He appointed a commission of nine cardinals to recommend guidelines for reform of the Church. In their report (1537) they pulled no punches. They were re-

5. Smith, *The Age of the Reformation*, 381.
6. Owen Chadwick, *The Reformation*, 1966, 273.

spectful, but they made it clear that in their opinion the great ills of the Church were traceable to former pontiffs who had all too readily abused the power of their office. Contarini, one of the commission, candidly urged a complete renovation of the Curia. He went so far as even to declare that the "Lutherans were entirely justified" in comparing the Holy See with the Babylonish captivity. The evil practices, which had alienated so many men, came from papal pretensions of absolute power. The rule of Peter and his successors was to be exercised, not according to any pope's own pleasure, "but in obedience to the rule of reason, of God's command, and to the law of love, referring everything to God, and doing all in consideration of the common good only."[7]

Pope Paul III was apparently sympathetic toward the reform of the entire Church organization by means of a general council. His efforts were not without some opposition or caution from certain prelates who feared curtailment of both power and income. One such warned him, "Commit yourself to nothing until it is agreed that the pope is absolute master of the council."[8] Under the prodding of the Emperor, Paul III did call a council, which eventually met at Trent, a little town in north Italy, but still within the confines of the Holy Roman Empire. The Germans were opposed to an Italian city because they distrusted papal influence. Even the Protestants were invited but refused to attend. One of Luther's reasons for his work *Against the Roman Papacy, an Institution of the Devil* (1545) was to justify the refusal of the Protestants to accept the invitation. The Council met in three separate sessions, 1545-1547, 1551-1552, and 1562-1563. During the second period the Protestants

7. Henry S. Lucas, *The Renaissance and the Reformation*, 1934, 646.
8. Chadwick, *The Reformation*, 273.

did send a delegation, which presented a confession of faith, but they refused to recognize the authority of the Council. It was the longest Council in the history of the Roman Church, as well as the last for over three hundred years. According to McBrien, "Until Vatican II, twentieth-century Catholicism was shaped more by the Council of Trent than by any other historically tangible event or force."[9]

In general review, it is quite apparent that there was throughout the whole course of the Council a more or less hidden struggle between the defenders of papal power and the conciliarists. Father Paul Sarpi, the Roman Catholic historian of Trent, judged that the Council was a failure, if not a fraud. The membership was packed with pro-papal, Italian yes-men, and Philip Schaff described the members of the Council as being "not distinguished for learning or piety, but were a set of wrangling monks and canonists and minions of the pope."[10] Another measure aimed at ensuring papal control of the Council was that of granting the initiative to the papal legates. While the Council was not under the immediate control of the pope, there was frequent communication from Rome, to the extent that the French ambassador jested of the Holy Ghost coming to Trent in the mailbags from Rome.[11] Pius IV (1559-1565), during the final sessions, was able to keep a majority of Italians on the Council, and in the final clash on papal supremacy he controlled the decisions by only seventy-one votes to sixty-six.

There were three basic tasks confronting those attending the Council of Trent: (1) the settlement of religious disputes

9. Richard P. McBrien, *Catholicism,* 2 volumes, 1980; Volume II, 635.
10. Philip Schaff, *History of the Christian Church*, Volume VIII, 279.
11. Smith, *The Age of the Reformation*, 391.

by doctrinal decisions; (2) the reform of ecclesiastical abuses; and (3) the discussion of a crusade against the infidel. Needless to say, the first two tasks were the cause of stormy debate. At times the controversy actually raged into physical violence. At one point dissension became so heated that one Bishop tore the beard of another. In the third period of the Council, contention over rules for the improvement of the convents waxed so hot that representatives of the various factions fought in the streets of Trent. During this third and final period it was obvious that the Council was under the control of the papacy. This was made evident by the request of the Council that all decrees should be confirmed by the pope. This was done by Pius IV one month after the Council ended on January 26, 1564, in the bull *Benedictus Deus*. Before the year was over, he issued another important bull, *Injunctum nobis*, which became the *Tridentine Profession of Faith*. Among the opening words of this profession of faith, to be recited publicly by all Bishops and beneficed clergy of the "Holy Roman Church," there is a startling statement with regard to the Church's authority to interpret the Holy Scriptures:

> I acknowledge the sacred Scripture according to that sense which Holy Mother Church has held and holds, to whom it belongs to decide upon the true sense and interpretation of the Holy Scriptures, nor will I ever receive and interpret the Scripture except according to the unanimous consent of the fathers.[12]

Among the other ecclesiastical traditions included in this profession of faith, which, according to the documents of the second Vatican Council (1962-1963), were still binding upon

12. Henry Bettenson, *Documents of the Christian Church*, 1947, 374.

Roman Catholics in the twentieth century, there were listed: the seven sacraments, transubstantiation, purgatory, veneration and invocation of saints, veneration also of relics, of images of Christ, of the ever-virgin mother of God, and of saints, and lastly, the power of indulgences. Those who embraced and received all the definitions and declarations of the "holy Council of Trent" were professing the "true Catholic faith" without which no one could be in a state of salvation. Required of those making this public profession was also the following credal oath: "I recognize the holy catholic and apostolic Roman Church as the mother and mistress of all churches; and I vow and swear true obedience to the Roman pontiff, and successor of blessed Peter, the chief of the apostles and the representative [*vicarius*] of Jesus Christ."[13]

Not only did the Council of Trent and the *Tridentine Profession of Faith* close the door to reconciliation with the Protestants, they also created what Trevor Jalland called "a siege mentality." As in times of severe national crisis constitutions are suspended and dictators with absolute authority are accepted, so among those remaining within the Roman camp the acceptance of papal absolutism became a condition of survival.[14] The analogy seems to be very appropriate, for there was a rapid reconstruction of doctrinal fortifications to counteract the threat from Protestantism. There was the imposition of a more centralized discipline. New religious orders came into existence, such as the Society of Jesus founded by Ignatius Loyola in 1540. In the constitution of this new order, the image of militant warfare was projected, and a special oath of allegiance to the Roman pontiff was a prerequisite.

13. Bettenson, *Documents of the Christian Church*, 375.
14. Trevor Gervase Jalland, *The Church and the Papacy*, 1944, 454.

About this same time, 1542 to be exact, the infamous Roman Inquisition was established. Related to the Inquisition, the Roman *Index of Prohibited Books* was promulgated. All in all, what was happening was that the old papal claims were being reasserted and shored up by a new coalition of forces and by a reformed papacy.

Rated high in this coalition of forces, which molded Roman Catholic thinking at the end of the sixteenth and beginning of the seventeenth centuries, must be the writings of Robert Bellarmine (1542-1621). During the high tide of the Counter-Reformation he was the principal theologian of the Society of Jesus. Next to the Council of Trent, his work has probably had more influence on the development of Roman Catholic theology in modern history than any other single factor. He was uncompromisingly ultramontane in his papal views. He viewed the Church in a monarchical manner, with the pope as supreme head and the Roman prelates as the aristocracy. The Roman pontiff is universal teacher of the Church and in this role is incapable of error. All councils are subordinate to him. He is to rule the Church with the plenitude of ecclesiastical jurisdiction, and he cannot be liable to judgment by others. As supreme ruler, he has the right to impose laws on all the faithful and to compel obedience even by means of the death penalty. Anyone familiar with the subsequent development of papal views of power, particularly toward the end of the nineteenth century, can hardly fail to notice how Bellarmine was in advance of his time.

Notwithstanding the "siege mentality" of the Counter-Reformation, the historical ebb and flow of events and forces throughout the seventeenth and eighteenth centuries contributed to a steady decline in papal power. Even the popes of the period, at least according to one sympathetic brief study of the papacy, "although themselves worthy men, were not for the most part men of great intellectual stature or strong character."[15] These were the years when the Roman Church was troubled by such movements as Jansenism, Gallicanism, and political Liberalism.

Jansenism, Gallicanism, and Liberalism

The Jansenists took their name from Cornelius Otto Jansen (1585-1638). The movement itself is not easy to explain. In some ways it resembled the Puritan and even the Quaker movements, which were Protestant and Enthusiast contemporaries. It might even be described as a sort of Roman Catholic revivalist phenomenon that gave expression to the need for a religion of the "inner soul." There was a stress upon conversion and the necessity and irresistibility of grace, that is, a sort of "Calvinizing of Catholicism." Had it not been for its open attack on the moral laxity of the Jesuits, and its tendency to play down the supremacy of the pope, it might have elicited no great alarm. Jansen's book *Augustinus*, published posthumously in 1640, was condemned by Pope Urban VIII (1623-1644) in 1642. Five propositions that supposedly summed up the Jansenist position were condemned by Pope Innocent X (1644-1655) in the bull *Cum occasione* (1653). One noteworthy result of the quarrel was the work of Blaise Pascal, the *Provincial Letters*, which added ammunition to the Jansenists in their battle against the Jesuits.

In certain ways Gallicanism looked like the old caesaropapism only in modern dress. The Byzantine emperors had seen their temporal power within a broad spiritual framework where they were charged with the supervisory protection of

15. James A. Corbett, *The Papacy, A Brief History*, 1956, 59.

the Christian faith. The new caesaropapism went a step further and tended to claim complete control over the church. Even papal power was to be made subject to the absolutism of the royal will. King Louis XIV (1643-1715) asserted this *droit de regale* in his conflict with Pope Innocent XI (1676-1689) over the drawing of revenues from vacant bishoprics and his claim to the right of nomination to these sees. Of course, Innocent XI contested the claim and declared invalid the acts of Bishops thus appointed. The French clergy supported the king and in 1692 stood behind the *Gallican Declaration*, which proclaimed that kings could not be subject to ecclesiastical power in temporal matters, and that they could not be deposed "directly or indirectly" by the authority of the Church. In this connection, it was also declared that subjects could not be dispensed from obedience nor absolved from the oath of allegiance to their kings by ecclesiastical decrees. Particularly noteworthy in this *Declaration* is Article II, which, while it conceded that "the plenitude of power in spiritual matters possessed by St. Peter and his successors" did remain, it did so in accordance with the decrees laid down by the Council of Constance.[16] Also, in Article IV, obvious restrictions were placed on the pope's magisterial office: "Although the pope has the chief voice in questions of faith, and his decrees apply to all churches and to each particular church, yet his decision is not unalterable unless the consent of the church is given."[17]

Similar sentiments, such as these contained in the *Gallican Articles*, were now becoming common. They were being expressed and bandied about by kings and scholars. One work, written under the pseudonym Febronius, which achieved

16. Bettenson, *Documents of the Christian Church*, 379.
17. Bettenson, 379.

widespread popularity and went quickly through a number of editions, advocated a constitutional theory of papal authority and urged the abandonment of all papal claims based on the false decretals. Within a few years of its appearance (1763) the "omnipotent" state appeared to have the papacy under tight control. In the case of Austria under Emperor Joseph II (1765-1790), the Church became little more than a department of the state and virtually every aspect of ecclesiastical life was subjected to government regulation. Joseph II even contemplated a complete renunciation of papal power.

In revolutionary France, the Church fared no better. The National Constituent Assembly voted for the Civil Constitution of the clergy, which provided for the election of Bishops and pastors by popular vote, denying any papal influence in their choice. Under the Directory and Napoleon, popes were imprisoned and cardinals were arrested and scattered. Unilaterally, Napoleon published the *Organic Articles*, which declared that all papal acts and bulls, also decrees of general councils, should be submitted to the government for approval.

Political Liberalism, which favored constitutional, representative government, also breathed out threatenings against any symptom of papal absolutism. But papal reaction was soon forthcoming. Claims of papal supremacy were by no means dead. The task was not an easy one. How best could the Roman Church secure its necessary power in the world to permit the continuance of its mission? This could scarcely be done without dealing with the basic question of the pope's position and the extent of his power.

Papal Infallibility

It was not until the nineteenth century, during the pontificate of Pius IX (1846-1878), that the question of the extent of papal power was officially settled. There can be little doubt, however, that it was Pius IX himself who maneuvered the whole thing.[18] In his first year as pope, on November 9, he issued an encyclical that declared his infallibility in matters dealing with faith and morals. Also worthy of mention is the fact that in this same letter he called Mary "immaculate." The dogma of the immaculate conception of Mary was proclaimed eight years later on December 8, 1854. Papal authority on the basis of tradition alone was the main force in the proclamation of this dogma. That such was the case is fully acknowledged by the Jesuit Schrader:

> It is an act to which no former pontificate can show a parallel; for the pope defined the dogma of his own sovereign authority, without the cooperation of a council; and this independent action involves practically, if not formally, another dogmatic definition, namely that the pope is infallible in matters of faith in his own person and not merely when presiding at a council.[19]

The next important step of Pius IX in preparation for the formal definition of the dogma of papal infallibility was the issuance of the *Syllabus of Errors*. This consisted of an authoritative condemnation of some eighty supposed errors that were prevalent in the modern world. On December 6, 1864, together with a special encyclical *Quanta Cura*, this *Syllabus* was sent to all the prelates of the Roman Church. The encyclical concluded with an expression of confidence in the power of the immaculate virgin, who is described as standing on the

18. One of the best studies in English dealing with the part played by Pius IX in the promulgation of the dogma of papal infallibility is that of J. B. Bury, *History of the Papacy in the 19th Century 1864-1878*, 1930.
19. Bury, *History of the Papacy in the 19th Century 1864-1878*, 50.

right hand of her Son, attired in a dress of gold with a cloak of divers colors, and as being the destroyer of all heresies in the universe. The religious phraseology of both documents reflects an obvious logical interdependence. Their contents are indispensable in tracing the development of views of papal power, for they reveal quite clearly that there was in fact little or no change from that of the medieval viewpoint. Ecclesiastical authority rests essentially in the pope, who is not only head of the Church, but is also above the state. The duty of governments is to protect the Church, and to compel and punish all who do not conform to its decrees. Papal power must not be limited to faith and morals. Even in the early years of the twentieth century the *Syllabus* was very much alive. In 1903 Cardinal Archbishop Fischer of Köln wrote in a pastoral letter to his clergy, "The *Syllabus of Errors* is a touchstone of our own time by which we can decide what agrees with Catholic truth and what contradicts it."[20]

Two days before issuing the *Syllabus*, Pope Pius IX made known to the Congregation of Rites the idea of holding a general council. There was a great deal of secrecy associated with the formative planning stages of this Council, and apparently it was only those on the inside who knew that the main objective of the Council would be the definition of papal infallibility. It was no mere coincidence that the date chosen for the opening of the Council was December 8, 1869. This was the same date as the dogma of the Immaculate Conception and the issuance of the *Syllabus*. Protestants were invited to attend, but in a manner fitting for "prodigal children." Protestantism was not to be discussed, for sentence was long ago pronounced. It was a *chose jugée*.[21] From the very beginning

20. Bury, *History of the Papacy in the 19th Century 1864-1878*, 44.

to the very end, the first Vatican Council was geared by papal machinations to railroad through the doctrine of infallibility.[22] There is hardly a better example of a *petitio principii* in all history. Where was the rationale in asking the Council to define a doctrine only the pope himself could define? As one French journalist observed, "it was a true master stroke to set the papal infallibility in operation before it is proclaimed as dogma."[23]

There was, of course, a great deal of controversy connected with the dogma of papal infallibility. Much of it dealt with the question of historical precedents. Archbishop Manning argued that since the doctrine was not mentioned between the fifth and the fifteenth century it meant that it must have been universally accepted. In the opposing camp, Döllinger argued exactly the opposite case, attributing the doctrine to forgeries and fictions. William Gladstone, in his book *Rome and the Newest Fashions in Religion*, made the statement, "The popes had kept up, with comparatively little intermission, for well nigh a thousand years their claim to dogmatic infallibility...."[24] Later he felt obligated to retract this statement admitting that it was made "without sufficient reflection" and "with culpable inadvertence."[25] After further research he changed his mind, exclaiming, "I do not deny to the opinion of papal infallibility an active, though a checkered and inter-

21. Bury, *History of the Papacy in the 19th Century 1864-1878*, 60.

22. As far as the "railroading" of papal infallibility is concerned, together with the work of J. B. Bury, Geddes MacGregor's book, *The Vatican Revolution*, 1958 merits consideration.

23. Bury, *History of the Papacy in the 19th Century 1864-1878*, 92.

24. Right Hon. W. E. Gladstone, M. P., *Rome and the Newest Fashions in Religion*, 1875, XXXIV.

25. Gladstone, 53.

mittent, life exceeding six centuries."[26] This would place the historical origins of the doctrine somewhere in the thirteenth century. The historical reliability of Gladstone's judgment is to be commended. It might be remembered that in chapter 2 it was mentioned that Brian Tierney's book *Origins of Papal Infallibility, 1159-1350*, which was published one hundred years after Gladstone's work, provided historical evidence that the association of infallibility with papal authority first came into play at the end of the thirteenth century. The gist of Tierney's research is worth recounting.

Writing strictly from a historian's point of view, Tierney sees no convincing evidence that the doctrine of papal infallibility formed any part of the theological or canonical traditions of the Roman Church before the thirteenth century. Pietro Olivi, a Franciscan master, first introduced it toward the end of the thirteenth century. Behind Olivi's thinking was the simple design to limit the capacity of future popes to cause any damage to the doctrines of the Church. He did this by insisting on the infallibility and "irreformability" of doctrinal decisions made by preceding popes. His arguments came into the limelight in the fourteenth century when certain Franciscans found it necessary in their struggle over the question of poverty to maintain that certain papal decrees were infallible and immutable. Later still the doctrine proved useful in combating conciliarism. In other words, the doctrine was invented in an atmosphere of dissidence to support one party against another. In similar vein, the popes themselves came to accept it, sometimes with reluctance, because it suited their convenience in the circumstances in which they found themselves. What Tierney has shown is that there is a wide gap between

26. Gladstone, *Rome and the Newest Fashions in Religion*, 54.

the medieval theologians and canonists, and the thinking of the first Vatican Council.

One of the most remarkable facts about the final outcome of the first Vatican Council in 1870 was the way the vote went on the doctrine of papal infallibility. By all outward appearances, and in marked contrast with the Council of Trent, the final favorable vote was a veritable landslide. Out of 535 prelates who voted, 533 cast affirmative responses. It should be mentioned that 106 members were absent. Among the absentees and those opposing the affirmative vote were Cardinals, Archbishops, Bishops and some of the Roman Church's leading historians – names such as Rauscher, Schwarzenberg, Conolly, Carboy, Hefele, Ketteler, Kenrick, Strossmayer, Cerot, Clifton, Dupanloup, and, not the least, the highly esteemed Dr. Döllinger. These men, along with others, represented no small storehouse of elaborate erudition. Of the 766 prelates in attendance, 541 were from Europe, and of these, 276 came from the Italian peninsula. Gertrude Himmelfarb makes the facetious comment: "In ecclesiastical statistics, it appeared that twenty learned Germans counted for less than one untutored Italian."[27] The day before the momentous vote was cast Dupanloup, one of the opposition leaders, persuaded those yet remaining in Rome to leave in a body and thus avoid casting a negative vote. He had already attempted to persuade the pope to exercise prudence and moderation and to postpone if possible any confirmation of the Council's decision with regard to the position and the power of the papal office. Archbishop Haynald of Hungary, in company with Dupanloup, left Rome on the eve of the final session. In the early morning

27. Gertrude Himmelfarb, *Lord Acton, A Study in Conscience and Politics*, 1952.

of the historic day, as Dupanloup was opening his breviary, Haynald leaned toward him and said: "Monseigneur, nous avons fait une grande faute" ("Monseigneur, we have made a great mistake.")[28]

Exactly what Haynald intended might be disputed. Did he express concern over being party to the opposition? Did he imply that they should have stayed and registered their negative vote? Whatever he meant, it made no difference to the outcome. On July 18, 1870, the decree contained in the document *The First Dogmatic Constitution Concerning the Church of Christ* was published and approved. The content of this decree merits close consideration. It begins with a brief introduction, followed by four comparatively short chapters. In each of them, with perhaps the exception of the last, which contains the big bone of contention concerning papal infallibility, the basic elements in the Petrine theory are all clearly proclaimed. The first chapter, titled "Of the Institution of the Apostolic Primacy in Blessed Peter," minced no words in its explicit claims. Clearly the statements focus upon Peter "alone" being the one to whom Christ the Lord spoke the words of *Matthew* 16:18-19. The decree concludes with the solemn anathema:

> If anyone, therefore, shall say that blessed Peter the apostle was not appointed the prince of all the apostles and the visible head of the whole church militant; or that the same directly and immediately received from the same our Lord Jesus Christ a primacy of honor only, and not of true and proper jurisdiction – let him be anathema.[29]

28. Trevor Gervase Jalland, *The Church and the Papacy*, 1944, 2.
29. MacGregor, *The Vatican Revolution*, 169.

The second chapter, headed with the words "On the Perpetuity of the Primacy of Blessed Peter in the Roman Pontiff," is no less explicit. Here is spelled out in unmistakable terms the doctrine of apostolic succession:

> That which the Prince of shepherds and great Shepherd of the sheep, Jesus Christ our Lord, established in the person of the blessed apostle Peter to secure the perpetual welfare and lasting good of the Church, must, by the same institution, necessarily remain unceasingly in the Church; which, being founded upon the rock, will stand firm to the end of the world. For none can doubt, and it is known to all ages, that the holy and blessed Peter, the prince and chief of the apostles, the pillar of the faith and foundation of the Catholic Church, received the keys of the kingdom from our Lord Jesus Christ, the Savior and Redeemer of mankind, and lives, presides, and judges, to this day and always, in his successors the Bishops of the holy see of Rome, which was founded by him, and consecrated by his book....
>
> If, then, any should deny that it is by the institution of Christ the Lord, or by divine right, that blessed Peter should have a perpetual line of successors in the primacy over the universal church, or that the Roman pontiff is the successor of blessed Peter in this primacy – let him be anathema.[30]

The third chapter, arguing in an apparently logical manner on the premises contained in the preceding two chapters, proceeds to define "The Power and Nature of the Primacy of the Roman Pontiff":

30. MacGregor, *The Vatican Revolution*, 171.

> All the faithful of Christ must believe that the holy apostolic see and the Roman pontiff possesses the primacy over the whole world, and that the Roman pontiff is the successor of blessed Peter, prince of the apostles, and is true vicar of Christ, and head of the whole church, and father and teacher of all Christians; and that full power was given to him in blessed Peter to rule, feed, and govern the universal church by Jesus Christ our Lord; as is also contained in the acts of the general councils and in the sacred canons.
>
> And since by the divine right of apostolic primacy the Roman pontiff is placed over the universal church, we further teach and declare that he is the supreme judge of the faithful, and that in all causes, the decision of which belongs to the church, recourse may be had to his tribunal, and that none may re-open the judgment of the apostolic see, than whose authority there is no greater, nor can any lawfully review its judgment. Wherefore they err from the right course who assert that it is lawful to appeal from the judgments of the Roman pontiffs to an ecumenical council, as to an authority higher than that of the Roman pontiff.[31]

Words could hardly be plainer. There could be no appeal from a papal judgment. No person or council could be permitted to review or modify the judgments of the Roman pontiffs. What purpose then was served by the council itself, or, for that matter, any future council? All that could be done was to rubber-stamp papal judgments. There was no room for compromise in the face of such claims. But the most stupendous pretension of all came in the fourth and last chapter "Concerning the Infallible Teaching of the Roman Pontiff":

31. MacGregor, *The Vatican Revolution*, 173, 175.

The first condition of salvation is to keep the rule of the true faith…in the apostolic see the Catholic religion and her holy and well-known doctrine has always been kept undefiled…. This see of holy Peter remains ever free from all blemish of error….

This gift, then, of truth and never-failing faith was conferred by heaven upon Peter and his successors in this chair, that they might perform their high office for the salvation of all….

Therefore, faithfully adhering to the tradition received from the beginning of the Christian faith, for the glory of God our Savior, the exaltation of the Catholic religion, and the salvation of Christian people, the sacred council approving, we teach and define that it is a dogma divinely revealed: that the Roman pontiff, when he speaks *ex cathedra*, that is, when in discharge of the office of pastor and doctor of all Christians, by virtue of his supreme apostolic authority, he defines a doctrine regarding faith or morals to be held by the universal church, by the divine assistance promised to him in blessed Peter, is possessed of that infallibility with which the divine Redeemer willed that His church should be endowed for defining doctrine regarding faith or morals; and that therefore such definitions of the Roman pontiff are irreformable of themselves, and not from the consent of the church.

But if anyone – which may God avert – presume to contradict this our definition – let him be anathema.[32]

In certain respects, the content of this document represents a concise statement of the result of the centuries-long development of the doctrine of papal power. What was implied a little earlier, that is, that there was no small degree of political

32. MacGregor, *The Vatican Revolution*, 175-179.

124

machinations behind the scenes before the document was accepted and published, has reference primarily to this last point. But even here, it might be argued that papal infallibility is simply a logical necessity in the light of the other claims. Be this as it may, in defense of those who opposed it, the doctrine could hardly be considered a tradition handed down from the beginning of the Christian faith. Certainly, in no way did it satisfy the three criteria of the Vincentian Rule. It was definitely not supported by "universality, antiquity, and consent." Even those most outspoken in its defense admitted that many had denied the doctrine.[33] In 1825 a British government commission had asked a panel of Irish Roman Catholic Bishops whether it was held that the pope was infallible. They responded that it was not part of Catholic teaching. Gladstone, in his work dealing with the Vatican Council, cited a long list of historical examples reaching from 1661 to 1825 in which Roman Catholic prelates and scholars directly and openly repudiated the doctrine of papal infallibility. They did this even though they were well aware that others within their Church held to the theory. One representative example of this attitude was Bishop Baines, who in 1822 wrote, "Bellarmine, and some other divines, chiefly Italians, have believed the pope infallible, when proposing *ex cathedra* an article of faith. But in England or Ireland I do not believe that any Catholic maintains the infallibility of the pope."[34]

Hence, unless one argues with tongue in cheek, no valid case can be made for believing that the doctrine of papal infallibility was a matter accepted by the entire Church in all places, and at all times.

33. MacGregor, *The Vatican Revolution*, 40.
34. Gladstone, *Rome and the Newest Fashions in Religion*, 48.

How then did such a doctrine come to be received by such an overwhelming margin of Council members? The case for the opposition had been presented with all the qualifications of the best scholarship. Urgings of practical expediency made little or no impact upon these men. They were concerned for truth. In spite of intolerable ridicule, some of them, like Bishop Strossmayer, stood their ground.[35] Others, such as the great Roman Catholic Church historian, Döllinger, refused to be intimidated. Even sixteen years later, after being excommunicated and under ecclesiastical threats of eternal damnation, he reported in writing that he had studied the matter further, and that he had found that it was to an even greater extent than he had supposed based on a mass of fictions and forgeries.[36] Not only did such men oppose the doctrine, but many of them were also persuaded that the Council itself "was neither legitimate in constitution, free in action, nor unanimous in doctrine."[37] But the fact remains, even if historical research provides indisputable evidence of the grossest forms of behind-the-scenes Machiavellianism, a pope presiding over the Council published the doctrine.

Thus July 18, 1870, marks a significant milestone in the theoretical development of papal power. That the doctrine was reconfirmed by later popes is evident in the following encyclicals: Pope Leo XIII, *Satis Cognitum* (1896); Pope Pius X, *Lamentabili* (1907); Pope Pius XII, *Mystici Corporis* (1943) and *Humani Generis* (1950). There can be absolutely no doubt about the intent of the decision of July 18, 1870. When the pope

35. See Appendix A.

36. MacGregor, *The Vatican Revolution*, 70.

37. John Emerich Edward Dalberg-Acton, *The History of Freedom and Other Essays*, 1967, 550.

speaks *ex cathedra*, in regard to doctrine, faith, or morals, he is infallible. The doctrine dare not be misunderstood. It is stated in unequivocal terms. Anyone presuming to contradict it falls under a solemn anathema. How easy it would be to dwell on the implications of this doctrine at greater length, for surely no one is infallible but God himself! Besides, all that is necessary to illustrate how false the doctrine is is to show from the history of the popes themselves how many times they have been guilty of moral and doctrinal errors.[38] Such matters will be touched upon briefly in the concluding chapter, but we must first consider the second Vatican Council, and its bearing upon the development of views of papal power.

The Second Vatican Council

According to Bishop Reuben H. Mueller, President of the National Council of Churches of Christ in the U.S.A., the second Vatican Council was "a new adventure in ecumenical cooperation" among the followers of the Lord Jesus Christ.[39] One of the cherished dreams of Pope John XXIII, who had called the Council, was the reunion of all "our brother Christians," the "separated brethren."[40] There can be little doubt that in contrast with the first Vatican Council and with Trent, the overall tone of the second Vatican Council appears to be quite moderate. The polemical tenor of those former Councils is conspicuously absent. For readers who share the theological perspective of the Reformation, the documents contain not a few surprises. For example, there is

38. Recommended on this subject is George Salmon, *The Infallibility of the Church*, 1914.

39. Walter M. Abbott, S. J., editor and translator: *The Documents of Vatican II*, 1966, xx.

40. *Documents*, xx, 6.

a notable emphasis upon Holy Scripture. Also the Council's "master and pivotal document on the nature of the church"[41] would appear, at least to a superficial reader, to mitigate the pronouncements of the first Vatican Council and of Trent, when it comes to the position and power of the pope. The fathers remain under the headship of "the successor of Peter," but they share in the "responsibility for the shepherding of the entire church of Christ."[42] The very first document, "Message to Humanity," published by the fathers, while it was issued "with the endorsement of the Supreme Pontiff," had nevertheless been sent to the Council by Pope John XXIII for discussion and "amendment," if necessary.[43]

In spite of the general conciliatory tone of the no less than 103,014 words that make up the documents of the second Vatican Council, the perceptive reader cannot fail to discern that there is in actuality no repudiation of Trent, or of the Vatican Council. If anything, when Trent or the first Vatican Council are mentioned, the emphasis is never critical. Quite the contrary, the second Vatican Council furthers "the work begun by the Council of Trent," or follows "in the footsteps of the first Vatican Council."[44] In the third chapter of the *Dogmatic Constitution of the Church*, Peter is represented as being placed over the other apostles, and as being "a permanent and visible source and foundation of unity of faith and fellowship."[45] Then, following very closely in the footsteps of the first Vatican Council, the reader is informed, "And all this teaching about the institution, the perpetuity, the force and

41. Abbott, *The Documents of Vatican II*, 1966, xv.
42. *Documents*, xvi.
43. *Documents*, 1, 3.
44. *Documents*, 37, 456.
45. *Documents*, 38.

reason for the sacred primacy of the Roman pontiff and of his infallible teaching authority, this sacred synod again proposes to be firmly believed by all the faithful."[46]

Should the reader fail to feel the full force of these words, there is ample reinforcement of their intent elsewhere. In the middle of Article 22 of Chapter 3, part of the decree reads, "in virtue of his office, that is, as vicar of Christ and pastor of the whole church, the Roman pontiff has full, supreme, and universal power over the church. And he can always exercise this power freely."[47] The basis of this claim is, as in the past, that the "Lord made Simon Peter alone the rock and key-bearer of the church (see *Matthew* 16:18-19)."[48] In consequence, the position and power of the popes remains the same. Each pope possesses "the prerogative of infallibility."[49] His doctrinal definitions of faith and morals are "irreformable."[50] As it was concluded in the first Vatican Council, so it is here also. The "therefore," as it appears in the chain of argument, is unmistakable; that is, because of the pope's infallibility these doctrinal definitions "need no approval of others, nor do they allow an appeal to any other judgment."[51] Certainly, Pope Paul VI, who assumed the papal throne during the sessions of the Council, was in full accord with these statements. In one of his first encyclical letters (*Ecclesiam Suam*, August 6, 1964) he wrote, "We bear the responsibility of ruling the church of Christ because we hold the office of Bishop of Rome and consequently the office of successor to the blessed apostle Peter, the bearer of the

---

46. Abbott, *The Documents of Vatican II*, 38.
47. *Documents*, 43.
48. *Documents*, 43.
49. *Documents*, 48.
50. *Documents*, 49.
51. *Documents*, 49.

master keys to the kingdom of God, vicar of the same Christ who made of him the supreme shepherd of His world-wide flock."[52]

So then, notwithstanding the apparent pastoral tone and the cultivation of an ecumenical spirit, there can be little doubt that the documents of the second Vatican Council follow in the tradition of Trent and the first Vatican Council. Even with regard to the question of infallibility, there is no significant modification. In case anyone might disagree on this score, he would be well advised to read Hans Küng's book *Infallible? An Enquiry*. As the title makes plain, Küng's main thesis is to subject the doctrine of infallibility to theological enquiry. What he has to say can hardly be misunderstood. He recognizes contrasting variations between the two Vatican Councils, but as touching infallibility, there is essential agreement.[53] The paradox in Küng's work is the antagonistic nature of his criticisms while he professes loyalty to the Roman Catholic Church. Out of a number of possible examples, the implications of the following are self-evident. Calling it his chief point, Küng writes, "That the greater the pope's efforts to take his teaching office seriously, the more they seem to take place at the expense of the credibility of that office and the inner cohesion of the church." Later, he states categorically, "The errors of the church's teaching office have been numerous and grave…they cannot be denied…."[54]

Küng's "hot potato" merits much closer consideration than this brief mention. His intellectual ability and personal courage arouse the greatest admiration. But while he deserves

52. Pope Paul VI, *Ecclesiam Suam*, Vatican Translation, 5.
53. Hans Küng, *Infallible? An Enquiry*, translated by Erich Mosbacher, 1972, 34, 56, 77, 102, *et al.*
54. Küng, 20, 27.

the highest praise, there is no valid sense in which he can be viewed as representing the authoritative doctrinal position of the official Roman hierarchy. In fact, Professor Küng was removed from his teaching post by the Vatican, which said that he could no longer be considered a bona fide theologian of the Roman Catholic Church. Regardless of the incisive nature of his criticisms, the second Vatican Council, together with the first and the Tridentine Canons, must remain the final word on Roman Catholic doctrine. And as has been clearly seen, these Councils, especially with regard to papal power, support unequivocally the whole Petrine theory. If there was any additional elucidation in theoretical development, it was with regard to the doctrine of papal infallibility. The second Vatican Council, then, is where this discussion must stop. What remains is a critical evaluation of the theoretical foundations of the Petrine theory. This means that the relevant passages of Holy Scripture will be the primary area of discussion in the next chapter. This is only fitting, since Scriptural arguments in support of the primacy and power of the Roman bishopric appeared incipiently as early as the fourth century, and continued right until the second Vatican Council.

6

Holy Scripture and Papal Claims

A S MIGHT readily be concluded from the preceding pages, papal claims have their roots in historical traditions, legends, and forgeries, laced together with the fanciful interpretations of certain passages of Holy Scripture. Of course, from the point of view of the Roman Church's authoritative pronouncements, the whole Petrine theory is viewed as nothing less than a Holy Spirit-inspired reflection of New Testament teaching. In this regard, not even the doctrine of papal infallibility would be exempted. However, as has been noted in the previous pages, not all Roman Catholic scholars have accepted these dogmatic assertions. Mention was made of men of the caliber of Karl Joseph van Hefele, Ignaz Döllinger, and Lord Acton. In the words of Lord Acton, papal infallibility was a doctrine unreachable by "the weapon of human reason," a doctrine which "resided in the inaccessible postulate rather than a demonstrable consequence of a system of religious faith."[1] In more recent times, theologians such as Hans Küng have tried to point out that "the case for the dogma of infallibility based on Scripture and tradition is plainly as meager as it is brittle."[2] Notwithstanding

1. John Emerich Edward Dalberg-Acton, *The History of Freedom and Other Essays*, 1967, 512.
2. Hans Küng, *Infallible? An Enquiry*, translated by Erich Mosbacher, 1972, 99.

such weighty opinions, the documents of the two Vatican Councils seem to indicate that even infallibility derives from logical deductions based upon premises assumed to be the result of correct interpretations of Scripture. Certainly, no papal supporter would argue otherwise. Anyway, regardless of whether papal infallibility is found implicitly or explicitly in Scripture, what is certain is that Scripture does figure over and over again in papal claims and this in itself is sufficient justification to review the pertinent passages.

Matthew 16:18-19

Without controversy, the first and the most important passage of Scripture upon which papal claims have been founded is *Matthew* 16:18: "And I say also unto you, that you are Peter, and upon this rock I will build my church; and the gates of Hell shall not prevail against it."[3]

The statement was made after Peter had answered the question that the Lord Jesus had put to his disciples: "But who do you say that I am?" (*Matthew* 16:15). Quite obviously, from the context, the answer to this question was of vital importance, for the truth contained therein was to form the foundation upon which the Lord was to build his church. Peter responded, "You are the Christ, the Son of the living God." The Lord then went on to say, "Blessed are you, Simon Barjona: for flesh and

3. Pope John Paul II, in his first public speech made on the ceremonial occasion of his coronation (Vatican City, October 22, 1978), reaffirmed unapologetically the claims of papal authority and the Petrine theory. He referred to the confession of Peter and the words of *Matthew* 16:16-18 and said, "The churchly aspect of the people of God draws its origins, is born indeed by the words of faith, and is bound to the man who pronounced them. You are Peter – rock, stone – and upon you, as upon a rock, I will build My church."

blood has not revealed it unto you, but my Father which is in Heaven" (*Matthew* 16:16-17). Then follow the words of verse 18, which literally could read: "But I also say to you, that you are Peter (*petros*, a stone), and upon this the rock (*petra*, the rock), I will build my church (*ecclesia*, congregation), and the gates of Hell shall not prevail against it."

Viewing the words of *Matthew* 16:18 in context, the most natural interpretation seems to focus upon Peter's correct identification of the Son of Man. Therefore, it is his confession of faith, when taken in its objective sense, which points to the rock. This would harmonize perfectly with many other passages of Holy Scripture (for example, *Deuteronomy* 32:4, 18; 2 *Samuel* 22:2, 3, 32; 23:3). The church is thus infallible, that is, "not liable to fail," because it is built upon the impregnable rock, that is, upon "Christ, the Son of the living God." Since it is built upon this rock "the gates of Hell" cannot prevail against it. How Peter could be such a rock is very difficult to imagine, for in the immediate context Peter is anything but infallible. Jesus Christ, the Son of the living God, had to say to him, "Get behind me, Satan: You are an offence unto me; for you savor not the things that be of God, but those that be of men" (*Matthew* 16:23).

From a comparison of other New Testament passages it is extremely difficult to conceive that Peter, or any of the apostles, had even the faintest knowledge of what is pretended in the Petrine theory. It must involve some very painful intellectual gymnastics to "prove" from the Bible that the Lord Jesus appointed Peter to be the first pope, thus establishing the papal throne. If anything, the very fact that the Lord appointed twelve apostles is itself good reason to cast doubts upon the whole idea of one, and only one, pope. As far as any throne was concerned, there were to be twelve, one for each of the apostles, but even this was to wait until the time when the kingdom of God would be established (*Matthew* 19:28).

It cannot be denied that Peter did manifest a comparative degree of prominence in the early chapters of the *Acts of the Apostles*, but such an admission hardly supports the Petrine theory. The very first chapter should point this out. It was not Peter who appointed Matthias to take the "bishopric" of Judas Iscariot; it was all the disciples of Christ acting together in prayer and in casting lots (*Acts* 1:20-26). In *Acts* 2, Peter's apparent position of leadership seems to derive more from his force of character than from any special divine appointment. The same appears to be the case in the succeeding narrative right up to chapter 12. Then, with the words: "And he went down from Judea to Caesarea, and there abode," Peter exits from Luke's account of the apostolic church (*Acts* 12:19). The remaining sixteen chapters of this first history book of the spread of the Gospel focus upon the ministry of Paul. Peter's one brief re-entry into the narrative in chapter 15 was primarily with a view to testifying in behalf of Paul's special apostleship to the Gentiles. Even after he spoke, the letters which were sent to the Christians in "Antioch and Syria and Cilicia" were sent from "the apostles and elders, with the whole church," not from Peter (*Acts* 15:23). There is not the slightest hint of any papal-like headship over any church anywhere in the New Testament. According to Paul, "the household of God," meaning the "congregation of God" is "built upon the foundation of the apostles and prophets, Jesus Christ himself being the chief cornerstone" (*Ephesians* 2:20). Also John, in the *Revelation*, describing the wall of the city of the heavenly Jerusalem, depicted it as having twelve foundations, each of which contains the names of the twelve apostles of the Lamb (*Revelation* 21:14). These references, and others such as *1 Cor-*

inthians 1:12; 15:5-11 and *2 Corinthians* 11:5, 28, leave no room for a doctrine that teaches that Peter possessed sole authority over the corporate body of believers.

Peter himself in neither his first nor his second *Epistle* left any indication that would lend credence to the Petrine theory. He identified himself as an apostle, not as the pope with ultimate authority over the people of God, and he left no doubt that Jesus Christ was the chief cornerstone of God's spiritual house (*1 Peter* 1:1; 2:5-8). Moreover, he classified himself as "an elder" among others who were "elders" (*1 Peter* 5:1). Further inferences along these lines can be found in the *Gospel of Mark*. Early tradition, such as Papias, asserted that Mark was both Peter's disciple and virtually his amanuensis in the composition of this second of the synoptic *Gospels*. Strange that the *Matthew* 16:18 episode is not recounted in *Mark*, if Peter was indeed the rock upon which the Christian church would be built. Yet, even more, why does Mark record the incidents concerning which of the twelve was the greatest, and the request of James and John to sit on the right hand and on the left, if Peter had already been granted the position as the pope (*Mark* 9:33-35; 10:35-45)?

There is also the account in *Acts* 15, where Peter manifested no papal prerogatives, and where, if anyone, James was the prominent spokesman. In this same connection, *Galatians* 2 describes Peter, along with James and John, as seeming to be a pillar in the church at Jerusalem. He is not even mentioned first. Beside this, Paul withstood Peter to his face, and publicly rebuked him for his fearful indiscretions at Antioch (*Acts* 15; *Galatians* 2:9-14). Such references hardly fit into the general scheme of the Petrine theory. What seems more consistent with the overall teaching of Scripture is the view that the rock be related to Peter's confession: "You are the Christ, the Son of the living God." Here, more than anywhere, is the basic essential truth upon which the congregation of the Lord would be built, and nothing would prevail against such a solid, infallible, foundational rock. As Paul told the Corinthian Christians, "For other foundation can no man lay than that is laid, which is Jesus Christ" (*1 Corinthians* 3:11).

Against all this, that is, against viewing *Matthew* 16:16-18 in the light of the New Testament as a whole, there yet remain the words, which complete the response of the Lord Jesus to Peter's confession of faith. From the authoritative documents that make up the dark "Magna Carta" of papal claims, it is obvious that they also figure prominently in the Petrine theory. The words appear in verse 19: "And I will give unto you the keys of the kingdom of Heaven: and whatsoever you shall bind on Earth shall be bound in Heaven; and whatsoever you shall loose on Earth shall be loosed in Heaven."

Binding and Loosing

There is obviously a figurative meaning to such language. This is corroborated by other Biblical passages (for example, *Isaiah* 22:22; *Revelation* 1:18; 3:7). Privilege and responsibility are clearly inherent in the possession and usage of such keys. Since the expression is modified by the phrase "the kingdom of Heaven," it apparently must be understood in close association with the significance of this phrase. Unto Peter were given privileges and responsibilities connected with the kingdom of Heaven. The further expanded qualification states, "And whatsoever you shall bind on Earth shall be bound in Heaven: and whatsoever you shall loose on Earth shall be loosed in Heaven." Before jumping to any hasty conclusions, or attributing too much singularly to Peter, comparison of the context of *Matthew* 18:18 should be made. There the same privileges and responsibilities were extended to all the disciples of the Lord Jesus.[4]

The phrase "the kingdom of Heaven" is found thirty-three times in the *Gospel of Matthew*. A linguistic variation "the kingdom of God" appears five times. There is really no essential difference between these two phrases, for where Matthew uses the one, the *Gospels* of *Mark* and *Luke* use the other. Matthew's distinctive preference for "the kingdom of Heaven" is apparently explainable by his intended readership. Since they were primarily Jewish, the substitution of the word "Heaven" for "God" was an acceptable literary device. For example, the *throne of Heaven* would mean the *throne of God*. In this same vein, an understanding of the historical context of the *Gospel* records helps to explain why the phrase is never adequately defined. Clearly implied in this phenomenon is the fact that no definition was ever needed, for the phrase obviously concerned something familiar to the Jews of that day. Their Holy Scriptures spoke of the time when the *God of Heaven* would set up his kingdom (*Daniel* 2:44; 7:14, 18, 27). Also, their Targums insert the phrase in contexts that leave no doubt that they expected to see an actual divine kingdom established on Earth (see *Zechariah* 14:9; *Micah* 4:7). Little wonder that we read in the *Gospel of Mark* of "Joseph of Arimathaea, an honorable counselor, which also waited for the kingdom of God" (*Mark* 15:43).

Anyone reading the *Gospel* narrative in an objective manner can hardly fail to notice the prominence given to the theme

---

4. *The Documents of Vatican II* (Chapter III, Article 22) acknowledge this fact. However, there is a significant qualification. This power was granted "to the college of apostles, joined with their head (*Matthew* 18:18; 28:16-20)."

of the kingdom of God. Thoughtful attention to the actual subject material not only impresses this fact upon the mind, but also prepares the reader for a better appreciation of what the Lord intended by the words spoken to Peter in *Matthew* 16:18-19. The *Gospel* record begins with the birth of the Lord Jesus Christ. He was of the house and lineage of King David. He was born to be "King of the Jews" and "a Governor that shall rule...Israel." He was the long-promised Messiah born to sit upon "the throne of his father David." All of this had been predicted by the mouth of the holy prophets "since the world began" (*Matthew* 1:17, 20; 2:2, 6; *Luke* 1:30-33, 70; 2:11). His preaching, like that of John the Baptist and the twelve apostles, had one main point: "Repent; for the kingdom of Heaven is at hand" (*Matthew* 3:2; 4:17; 10:7). His great Sermon on the Mount was permeated with an emphasis upon the divine kingdom (*Matthew* 5:3, 10, 19, 20; 6:10, 13, 33; 7:21). Apart from true repentance, and meeting the spiritual qualifications, there was no hope for entering the kingdom, even for those who had a prior claim through physical descent from Abraham (*Matthew* 3:7-9; 8:11, 12; *John* 3:1-8). He chose twelve men as apostles, official representatives of his kingship, and they were promised the occupancy of twelve thrones ruling over the twelve tribes of Israel at the time of the consummation of his kingdom (*Matthew* 19:28). They were given authoritative responsibilities commensurate with their exalted privileges, among which the words of *Matthew* 18:18-19 have their setting. "Verily I say unto you, whatsoever you shall bind on Earth shall be bound in Heaven; and whatsoever you shall loose on Earth shall be loosed in Heaven. Again I say unto you, that if two of you shall agree on Earth as touching any thing that they shall ask, it shall be done for them of my Father which is in Heaven."

What the notion of this authoritative binding and loosing means can be gleaned from both Biblical and contemporary rabbinical sources. John Lightfoot wrote of the possibility of producing thousands of examples of this particular concept from rabbinical writings. He asked, "To think that Christ, when he used the common phrase, was not understood by his hearers in the common and vulgar sense, shall I call it a matter of laughter or of madness?"[5] From the examples cited from the school of Shammai, and from the school of Hillel, both of which were influential in the days of Christ, the meaning is quite clear. The phrase was used with reference to doctrines and judgments, and the idea of binding conveyed the meaning of forbidding, and loosing signified permission. That such was indeed the intention may be inferred from such New Testament references as *Matthew* 13:52; 23:13; and *Luke* 11:52. The last reference is particularly noteworthy, for it connects the concept of "the key of knowledge," that is, the truth concerning entrance into the kingdom of God. Peter and the other apostles were instructed in this matter, and they exercised their binding and loosing authority frequently throughout the early history of the book of *Acts* (see *Acts* 2:37-47; 3:1-26; 4:1-12; 5:17-32; 15:1-29; 21:17-26).

One interesting footnote with regard to the exercise of the divine knowledge granted to Peter and the other apostles comes out when closer attention is paid to the verbal construction in *Matthew* 16:19 and 18:18. For those not familiar with Greek, any good interlinear version should serve to bring out what is highly noteworthy. To borrow from the literal English translation of Alfred Marshall, the pertinent part is rendered: "Whatever you bind on the Earth shall be having been bound

5. John Lightfoot, *Hebrew and Talmudical Exercitations*, 1859, 234-240.

140

in the heavens, and whatever you loose on the Earth shall be having been loosed in the heavens." *Matthew* 18:18, other than being in the plural form, could be rendered in the same way. Keeping in mind that binding means "to forbid," and loosing means "to permit"; also that the exercise concerns doctrinal judgments, the interpretation of the words seems quite clear. Whatever the apostles were forbidding or permitting, they were doing so because it had already been forbidden or permitted in Heaven. In simple terms, their teaching reflected the principles of the kingdom of Heaven. They were a very special group of people, the foundation of the household of God, called out of darkness into God's marvelous light, entrusted with the oracles of God, and thus, because of their privileges, they were able to make known the will of God. C. B. Williams has rendered these two verses as follows: "I will give you the keys of the kingdom of Heaven, and whatever you forbid on Earth must be what is already forbidden in Heaven, and whatever you permit on Earth must be what is already permitted in Heaven. I solemnly say to you, whatever you forbid on Earth must be already forbidden in Heaven, and whatever you permit on Earth must be already permitted in Heaven."[6]

John 20:23, John 21:15-17, Luke 22:32

While we are touching upon the verbal construction of these verses, this might be a good place to mention the words recorded in *John* 20:23: "Whose soever sins you remit, they are remitted unto them; and whose soever sins you retain, they are retained." This verse, along with the two passages in *Matthew*, has been used to provide Scriptural sanction

6. Charles B. Williams, *The New Testament, A Translation in the Language of the People*, 1950, 47, 51.

for the sacerdotalism of the Roman Church. However, the perfect tense, when rendered correctly, prohibits any concept of men being able to forgive sins on behalf of God. When translated literally, *John* 20:23 could read as follows: "Whose soever sins you forgive (aorist, active, subjunctive), they have been forgiven (perfect, passive, indicative): whose soever sins you retain, they have been retained" (tenses correspond as before). Clearly, the basic intent is akin to that in the *Matthew* passages. In simple terms, the Lord taught the disciples to treat as forgiven those who were already forgiven by God. Such a paraphrase gives the Greek perfect tense its full grammatical force, namely the idea of the continuance of completed action.[7]

Understanding *John* 20:23 and the verses in *Matthew* as suggested makes the exercise of "the keys of the kingdom" much easier to appreciate. It also makes papal pretensions all the more ludicrous. The apostles were elevated to the rank and privilege enjoyed by the scribes, but they were not to perpetuate the abuses of the scribes. They were to teach the Word of God and not to make additions and substitutions taken from the doctrines and commandments of men (*Mark* 7:1-13). They were not to exceed their authority. They were interpreters of God's Word, and as such they were to persuade men to do the will of God on Earth as it was done in Heaven (*Matthew* 6:10). No pope, no priest, or no man for that matter, can go beyond this commission. What sheer arrogant nonsense for any human ecclesiastical authority to pretend that, through its own power or holiness, it can determine who enters, or who does not enter, the kingdom of God! Apart from meeting the conditions established by God himself, and so clearly

7. A. T. Robertson, *A Grammar of the Greek New Testament*, 1915, 893.

set forth in his Word, it is wasted breath for any man to claim the power to forgive sins. Worse, it is blasphemy! "Who can forgive sins but God only?" (*Mark* 2:7-12). Paul warned the Corinthian Christians "not to think of men above that which is written," and Peter wrote to the Christians in Asia Minor to speak according to "the oracles of God" (*1 Corinthians* 4:6; *1 Peter* 4:11).

Beside *Matthew* 16:16-19, there are probably two other passages in Holy Scripture that ought to be mentioned in relation to papal claims. They are *John* 21:15-17, and *Luke* 22:32. John Henry Newman is quoted as saying, "The long history of the contest for or against the pope's infallibility has been but a growing insight into the meaning of these three texts."[8] The reader, of course, must study these texts for himself, but it surely involves some fancy exegetical footwork (hardly "growing insight") to interpret them as teaching the conferral upon Peter of absolute episcopal jurisdiction over the other apostles, over the whole church, and over the whole world. The words of *John* 21:15-17: "Feed my lambs...feed my sheep," when viewed in context, describe a special renewal of Peter's apostleship after the humiliation of his threefold shameful denial of knowing his Lord (*John* 18:15-27). They do imply a teaching ministry, but then the other apostles were also commissioned to go and "teach all nations" (*Matthew* 28:19). As far as *Luke* 22:32 is concerned, the context once again bears consideration. At least it makes it very clear that Peter was no infallible rock (compare verses 33-34). The Lord forewarned Peter that he would be guilty of denying him three times. Therefore, the Lord uttered words suited to encourage Peter,

8. John Schulte, *Roman Catholicism, Old and New from the Standpoint of the Infallibility Doctrine*, 1876, 311.

certainly not to appoint him as exalted, infallible head over the other apostles.

What more can be said on this subject? Each reader must think carefully about the whole matter for himself. If the Lord Jesus Christ had intended to establish the supreme authority of Peter, and to have that authority perpetuated in the Bishops at Rome, then it is only reasonable to assume that he would have distinctly informed his followers. So important an office would surely have been mentioned in the clearest of terms. Other sacred offices are set forth in Holy Scripture, yet strange silence prevails with regard to that which would be the highest of all. There is not one jot or tittle, anywhere from *Genesis* to *Revelation*, about any man being a regal-sacerdotal king, who as vicegerent of Christ rules over the visible church upon the Earth. Such a thing just cannot be found in Holy Scripture. From whence then does it come? In the light of what has been set forth in the preceding pages, only one answer seems plausible. It is that which the Lord Jesus Christ and both Peter and Paul inveighed against, namely, "the tradition of men" (*Matthew* 15:1-9; *Mark* 7:9-13; *Colossians* 2:8; *1 Peter* 1:18). As it was with the Jews in the Old Testament dispensation, so it was with the Church of Rome under the New; both elevated their man-made traditions above the written Word of God. If the Lord condemned the former, would he not have condemned the latter? Men have not changed, be they Jew or Gentile. The warnings of Scripture are as valid today as when they were first written.

"Beware lest any man spoil you through philosophy and vain deceit, after the tradition of men, after the rudiments of the world, and not after Christ."

7

Conclusion

JAROSLAV PELIKAN, borrowing from Sir Winston Churchill's description of the Soviet Union, called the Roman Church "a riddle wrapped in a mystery inside an enigma."[1] The words appropriately summarize my sentiments with regard to the Roman papacy. In broad outline, the historical origins of papal power reach back to as early as the fourth century. The theoretical and practical development of that power extends over the centuries that followed, all the way to the twentieth century. The authority of the Bishop of Rome progressed from the diocese of his own city, where it had definite limits, to that of universal bishop over the whole Earth. At times, particularly during the Middle Ages, papal power became virtually a super-power without equal even in temporal matters. Yet, all along, its foundational claims were supposedly spiritual in nature.

The Constantinian Temptation

I use the word "supposedly," because it seems apparent that in the transitional developments of papal power there was an insidious shift of emphasis. Without realizing what was happening, the church lost the dynamic of its spiritual power in exchange for a mess of political pottage. The nature

1. Jaroslav Pelikan, *The Riddle of Roman Catholicism*, 1959, 13.

of the change was gradual, probably having its roots in the circumstances and consequences surrounding the decline and fall of the Roman Empire. On a much smaller scale similar developments have been witnessed many times throughout the history of Christianity. Ecclesiastical organizations are governed by fallible men, and as Lord Acton so laconically put it, "Power tends to corrupt, and absolute power corrupts absolutely." Running together with this constant tendency, there is the subtle process wherein a militant movement loses its vitality because loyalty switches inconspicuously from its ideals to its institutions.

Perhaps the spirit of this process can be illustrated by the fable of the dog that lost its bone by grabbing for what it thought was a bigger bone. What happened was that the dog came to the side of a pond and there, looking down, saw reflected on the surface of the water a dog holding a bone in its mouth. The imaginary bone looked much bigger and better. So it let go of the one it had in order to grasp at the one it thought was better. The moral is obvious. In reaching for temporal and political power, the papacy lost the primary ministry of the church, that is, it lost the Gospel. Maybe this is what Dante had in mind when in the nineteenth canto of his *Inferno* he wrote,

> *Ah! Constantin, di quanto mal fu matre,*
> *Non la tua conversion, ma qualla dote*
> *Che da te prese il primo ricco patre!*

> Alas! Constantine, how much misfortune you caused,
> Not by becoming Christian, but by that dowry
> Which the first rich father accepted from you![2]

2. Dante Alighieri, *La Divina Commedia*, 1959, 125.

146

Of course, the institutionalized papacy of the Middle Ages could hardly be expected to view itself as being caught in the interplay of historical forces which produced radical changes in its structure and ministry. On the contrary, its inherent bias was to view its origins and development as being the practical outworking of divine doctrinal concepts. Such doctrines, as my research has indicated, were themselves subject to development and systematization. They originated supposedly in the teachings of Holy Scripture, with *Matthew* 16:18-19 being the chief cornerstone. Building upon wild inferences from this passage, champions of papal pretensions bolstered their claims by subtle arguments, and by the use of cleverly fabricated forgeries. Essentially, the end result was the Petrine theory, which was eventually fitted with the supreme capstone of papal infallibility. This meant that according to official Roman Catholic dogma, the pope is nothing less than God's vicegerent on Earth, who when speaking *ex cathedra* on matters dealing with faith and morals, is under the direct infallible control of the Holy Spirit.

Truth and History

Having summarized very briefly the scope of my findings, there are two things I would like to do before concluding: (1) raise the question of the truthfulness of papal claims; and (2) touch upon the historical facts, which show that popes have erred. Of course, both points are obviously related. With regard to the first one, I readily admit that discussion might not be as simple as it seems. However, it cannot be shelved for a number of reasons. In my case, these reasons stem primarily from a personal bent of mind, which functions in a framework where objective Christian truth is very important. I believe wholeheartedly that the Christianity taught in the Holy Scriptures is true. Such a belief produces a reflex reaction that causes me to question any form of Christianity that goes beyond what is written in Holy Scripture. That the papal claims do go beyond Scripture cannot be denied. Herein lies the difficulty in testing the truthfulness of papal claims. For one thing, it involves an excursion into a sort of forbidden no man's land between history and theology. This, in turn, leads to a frustrating experiment in attempting to "unscrew" the inscrutable. I know that this must sound somewhat facetious but, in reality, the quest does indeed lead very early to a basic fallacy in logic known as "circular reasoning." Let me try to explain. From the Roman Catholic point of view, the truthfulness of papal claims rests upon the statements of Scripture, such as *Matthew* 16:18-19. In turn, the statements of Scripture are accredited only by the Magisterium of the Roman Church, whose infallible voice is the pope. Papal hegemony/infallibility is true because the Bible says Christ said he would build his Church on Peter and gave him the keys of the kingdom. And the Biblical statements are true because the infallible Magisterium of the Church says they are. The circle is complete; but the argument is unsound. One cannot use one proposition to prove a second, and then use the second to prove the first. In such a scheme neither proposition rests on anything solid.

Sometimes it is argued that the preceding deadlock can be terminated simply by recognizing that the Roman Church is older than other churches. Even if such a claim were historically true, which it is not, there still remains an enormous chasm to cross before arriving at the Petrine theory. From the *Acts of the Apostles* we learn that there were in existence many churches that antedated the founding of a church at Rome. Moreover, such a line of argument would lead to the church at Jerusalem being the oldest church (see *Acts* 2:47). What would this prove? The prominence and prestige of the Roman Church came not because it was the earliest of the churches. Churches were established in Greece before any were in Italy. Does this prove that the Greek Orthodox Church was earlier than the Roman Church? From a strictly historical perspective they had simultaneous and mingled origins. Like a flowing stream, which strikes a rock and divides, neither resultant can claim to be the exclusive original. A similar problem prevails even with regard to Luther and Calvin. To argue that they are the founders of the evangelical tradition is as ridiculous as if one were to argue that the American ideal of government began with the protest against Nazism. The essential question cannot be resolved as long as there persists circular argument. Without Holy Scripture as the axiom and final court of appeal, there is no resolution.

The second point, regarding the question of papal errors, is not as abstruse as the first one. If it were, then Hans Küng would hardly have written, "The errors of the church's teaching office have been numerous and grave...."[3] Apparently they are of such a nature that he could refer to them as "the classical errors now widely admitted...."[4] Again, I find these statements to be dumbfounding. It is not that I would disagree with them. On the contrary, I would agree, but they are made by one who considers himself loyal to the Roman Catholic Church, and yet who makes statements which fly right into the face of the authoritative definitions of Roman Catholic dogma. According to the Tridentine Canons and the two Vatican Councils, the Roman Church not only professes to be the one true church, it

3. *Hans* Küng, *Infallible? An Enquiry*, translated by Erich Mosbacher, 1971, 27.
4. Küng, 27.

also postulates that "In the apostolic see the Catholic religion and her holy and well-known doctrine has always been kept undefiled...ever free from all blemish or error...."[5] What is more, it is clearly stated that from this teaching, "no one can deviate without loss of faith and of salvation."[6] Talk about a dilemma! Küng tells his readers that "It is impossible honestly to deny objective errors committed by the Church's teaching office both ordinary and extraordinary,"[7] and yet, the Church's teaching office personified in the popes claims freedom from all blemish and error. Moreover, anyone contradicting this doctrine puts himself immediately under a solemn anathema.

Let the reader grasp the weight of the dilemma. In the final analysis, there is no escaping the conclusion that submission to the Roman Church must rest upon an act of private judgment. (And the right of private judgment is, of course, denounced by the Roman Church.) But how can anyone submit, if the papacy has indeed been guilty of "extraordinary" errors? By way of a few examples, take first the case of Pope Liberius (352-366). Not only did he subscribe to a heretical Arian creed, but he also anathematized Athanasius, the great defender of the Nicene Creed. Also Pope Zosimus (417-418) first pronounced Pelagius to be orthodox, and then reversed his judgment. Then there was Honorius (625-638) who was condemned as a heretic by both a council and by several subsequent popes. There was the case of Hadrian II (867-872) declaring civil marriages to be valid, and then Pius VII (1800-1823) condemning them as invalid. Along similar lines, Eugene IV (1431-1447) condemned Joan of Arc to be burned alive as a witch, while Benedict XV

5. Geddes MacGregor, *The Vatican Revolution*, 175-179.
6. MacGregor, 173, 175.
7. Küng, *Infallible? An Enquiry*, 144.

(1914-1922) in 1919 declared her to be a saint. The suppression and the restoration of the Jesuits were both brought to pass by papal decrees. The recommendation and the condemnation of Bible reading likewise fell under papal *pronunciamentos*.

One of the more notorious examples of extraordinary, and, it might be added, shameful erroneous actions of the papal Curia was the condemnation of Galileo. The Sacred Congregation of the Holy Office, created in 1542, had the authority to ban books judged harmful to the faith and morals of communicants. The catalogue of books known as the *Index of Prohibited Books* waged war on the Copernican theory for over two centuries. The *Index* of 1704 even contained the prohibition against "all books that teach the mobility of the Earth or the immobility of the Sun."[8] Anyone who has made a serious attempt to look at this side of papal power can scarcely charge Küng with exaggeration when he declares that, "In every century the errors of the church's teaching office have been numerous and indisputable...."[9] Beside these historical examples, which could be expanded to fill many pages, what of the gross wickednesses, intrigues, and immoralities of many of the popes?[10] I prefer to omit discussion of this side of papal history. Reliable works are readily available for the interested

8. George Salmon, *The Infallibility of the Church*, 1914, 237. A good guide to the history of prohibitory indexes is the work by George Haven Putnam, *The Censorship of the Church of Rome*, 2 volumes, 1907.

9. Küng, *Infallible? An Enquiry*, 28. Küng, of course, cites many examples to support this assertion. There are other works that deal particularly in greater detail with this matter – for example Loraine Boettner, *Roman Catholicism*, 1964.

10. The reader need not look in Protestant "anti-Catholic" books for a detailed account of this aspect of papal history. It is described with surprising frankness in a book displaying the Imprimatur of Cardinal Spellman: Glen D. Kittler, *The Papal Princes*, 1960.

reader. I have said enough. What remains is my bewilderment. How, in the face of undeniable and indisputable historical facts, can any sane and sensible person make that act of private judgment (surely only by some form of intellectual suicide) wherein he submits to what the Roman Church teaches concerning papal power?

The Unbridgeable Chasm between Christianity and the Papacy

This rather vehemently worded question might provide a convenient exit to end this study. Little can be gained by a further multiplication of words. Besides, I have accomplished my objective. After thousands of pages of research, I have arrived at answers, which satisfactorily have enabled me to cross the gap between the simple straightforward teachings of Holy Scripture and the *de facto* power of the hierarchical body that governs the Roman Church. However, in concluding, let me borrow and adapt a somewhat far-out imaginary parable, which should serve to summarize my overall sentiments. In order to get the point across with greater force, let me personalize the parable, and let me revert to the setting of being a kind of tour leader in and around Vatican City.

Just suppose that while I am leading my small party around the magnificent splendors of Vatican City, an uninvited odd-looking creature attaches himself to our group. In spite of his nondescript features, he is polite, and explains that he is making some exploratory inquiries concerning famous places on planet Earth. He makes it very clear that he will be no trouble, and that he will not be with us long, for he has a spaceship hovering outside waiting to whisk him away to his next appointment. All he really wants, so he informs us, is to know the real meaning and the essential significance of the buildings, the statues, and the activities of the multitudes of people who surround us. At that point, a passer-by, who had been struck by the odd appearance of our extraterrestrial visitor, and who had stopped to listen to what he had to say, intrudes into the conversation. Gesturing with an all-encompassing sweep of his hand, and with reassuring candor, he blurts out, "This is the Christian religion." Then, continuing, he exclaims that all that is really needed to find an adequate explanation of what it all signifies is a copy of the New Testament, which can be obtained in the authorized tourist shop across the square.

Not being the kind of alien to waste time, he allows his computer-like brain to make one further sweep of the surroundings, expresses his appreciation, exits with amazing speed through the main doors, visits the tourist shop, picks up a copy of the New Testament, and within seconds is back at the controls of his saucer-like spacecraft. After blast off, he begins to feed the data from his observations into the central information bank, and acting on the word of the earthlings, with a view to registering an explanatory summary of his visit, he files the facts taken from the New Testament into the terminal marked Comparative Analysis. Curious concerning the results, he pushes the print-out button, and after a few bleeps and blurps a message appears on the screen: RELATIONSHIP – IF – ANY – REMOTE: POSSIBLE – HUMAN – ERROR – INSERTION – OF – WRONG – BOOK.

True enough, the space-traveling visitor is imaginary, but as mentioned, he was introduced by way of analogy simply to highlight my own sentiments over the great chasm between the ecclesiastical colossus headed by the papacy at Rome, and that church described in the New Testament. Nevertheless, somehow or other, I was determined to make an attempt to

153

bridge the gap. In certain respects, I never lost my bewilder-ment, for the deeper my research took me, and the further I was removed from the days of the New Testament apostles, the bridge became shakier. Particularly was this the case as I wandered around in the no-man's-land between theology and history during the Middle Ages. However, among the political and religious vicissitudes of that period, I was able to discover sufficient landmarks to keep me headed in the right direction. And it was there, more than anywhere else that I began to comprehend both the theoretical foundations and the actual historical forces that shaped the development of papal power. I had one great advantage over our imaginary space traveler. I had more data than he had. Naturally, as can readily be expected, that can make a world of difference as far as drawing the right conclusion is concerned. Should he ever return, perhaps he might happen upon someone who could share with him a few excerpts from this study which, when fed into his computer, might possibly print out: TIME + HISTORICAL FORCES = RADICAL TRANSFORMATION. RESULT = HYBRID RELIGION.

APPENDIX A

The First Vatican Council

Introduction

LISTED among the opponents of the definition of papal infallibility at the first Vatican Council were some of the most scholarly and cultured prelates of that day, such as Dupanloup, Darboy, Hefele, Kenrick, Ketteler, Maret, Rauscher, Schwarzenberg, and Strossmayer. To these could be added historians and writers such as Döllinger, Gratry, Montalembert, and Lord Acton. It reflects an extreme bias indeed to dismiss the arguments of the opposition under the catch-all word "inopportuneness." Yes, there were many at the Council who did argue that the definition should be delayed because it would widen the gap between the Roman Catholic Church and the modern world, but there were a notable number that rested their case solidly on historical and Biblical grounds. And on such grounds, as Bishop Hefele protested, "The question was not one of being opportune or inopportune; infallibility was simply not true."[1]

One of the most outspoken opponents of the doctrine of papal infallibility was Josef Strossmayer. J. B. Bury, who succeeded Lord Acton as the Regius Professor of Modern History at Cambridge University, called him "the most courageous man

---

1. Fredrik Nielsen, *The History of the Papacy in the XIXth Century*, translated by Arthur James Mason, 2 volumes, 1906; Volume II, 310.

at Rome."[2] James Cardinal Gibbons, himself a participant at the Council, described him as "the most eloquent prelate of the Council."[3] His scholarship was self-evident, and in spite of denigrating stories about his personal life that some of his opponents were wont to spread abroad, his character was irreproachable.

He was a man who did not mince words. Several of the turbulent scenes that disturbed the peace of the Council were due to his speeches. In one debate he spoke out for reform, not only in the College of Cardinals, but also in the See of Peter itself. He went so far as to call Canon Law "that confusion of Babel," and he made no secret of his disapproval of the abuse the infallibilists made of quotations from the Bible. In another speech, when he tried to counter anti-Protestant generalizations, which had been presented in the introduction to the schema "Of the faith," he was interrupted by the president of the Council and told, "This is not the place to praise Protestants." His manner had been courteous, but he had dared to declare that the judgment against the Protestants was consistent "neither with truth nor charity."

As this particular speech continued, he was met with angry shouts from various sides of the assembly: "Shame, shame, down with the heretic." Others, infuriated by his words, muttered such sentiments as: "He is Lucifer, anathema, anathema," and "He is another Lucifer, let him be cast out." When Monsignor Place, Bishop of Marseilles, spoke up and said, "I do not condemn you," he was met with the response: "All of us, all of us condemn him!"

2. J. B. Bury, *History of the Papacy in the 19th Century*, 1930, 117.
3. James Cardinal Gibbons, *A Retrospect of Fifty Years*, 2 volumes, 1916; Volume I, 26.

Obviously, there was more behind such outbursts than the mere question of misrepresenting Protestantism. Strossmayer had become a marked man. His leadership among the anti-infallibilists was common knowledge. In this same speech he had dared to criticize the restrictions that shackled the order of procedure, and also to condemn the principle that propositions of faith could be decided by counting noses. A majority of votes, in his mind, was no way to determine doctrine that would "bind the conscience of the Catholic world on condition of eternal life and death."[4] In his opinion the Council lacked both liberty and truth. He was not alone in this opinion. Others, such as Archbishop Kenrick, said virtually the same thing. Kenrick, according to Gibbons, "was violently opposed to the definition, not only because he considered its inopportuneness, but because he did not see that it was part of the deposit of faith...."[5]

Besides Kenrick's spoken words during the Council, we have the complete, seventy-five page text of the speech, which he had intended but was unable to give, due to a sudden unexpected shutting off of the debate. In spite of the rules, which forbid the printing of speeches under severe penalties, he nevertheless, in his own words, "deemed best that his divine right of expressing his views on this momentous business to his fellow-bishops, and to others who are entitled to an interest in the Council, should be exercised through the press."[6] After setting forth Biblical and historical arguments in opposition to the doctrine of papal infallibility, he concluded by making

4. Joannes Dominicus Mansi, *Sacrorum Conciliorun Nova et Aniplissima Collectio*, 1961, Volume 51, 72-77. Also Nielsen, II, 351.

5. Gibbons, *A Retrospect of Fifty Years*, I, 32.

6. Peter Richard Kenrick, "Speech in the Vatican Council," Leonard Woolsey Bacon, editor, *An Inside View of the Vatican Council*, 92.

reference to "trickery" which stacked the deck in favor of those who were determined to exalt the authority of the pope.[7] In Hans Küng's words, "As painful and embarrassing as it may be to admit, this Council resembled a well organized and manipulated totalitarian congress rather than a free gathering of free Christian people."[8]

"Trickery" might be judged too prejudicial a word, but the papal bull *Multiplices inter*, which became the parliamentary handbook for the Council, was clearly on the side of the infallibilists. For example, only the pope had the initiative to propose topics, and only he possessed the prerogative to nominate the officers of the Council. Add to this the predisposition of loyalty the prelates felt toward the pope as the head of the Roman Catholic Church, and it becomes easier to understand why the questions of liberty and truth could be overlooked and how debate could drift to the soft-ground of inopportunism or inexpediency.

In Lord Acton's words, the result was that the majority came to a mind-set, which was "acting less from conviction than by command."[9] Or, as he wrote in another place, "Authority must conquer history."[10] What Acton meant, of course, as Bishop Hefele had so frankly stated during the debates, was that no genuine historical document could be found which implied that the ancient church had believed in the pope's infallibility. Bishop Richard V. Whelan described this mind-set in a letter he wrote to Bishop Dupanloup: "I am convinced that all the

---

7. Kenrick, "Speech in the Vatican Council," 164.

8. August Bernhard Hasler, *How the Pope Became Infallible*, 1981, 12.

9. Lord Acton, "The Vatican Council," H. A. MacDougal, *Lord Acton on Papal Power*, 1973, 177.

10. Lord Acton, "The Vatican Council," 145.

arguments which can be accumulated will have no effect with those who favor this doctrine. In one way or another they reject everything. Reasons mean nothing. Facts count for nothing.... They want it; they have decided on it; nothing can prevent it (humanly)."[11]

Another speech that summarized the Biblical and historical arguments appeared under the name of Bishop Strossmayer in an Italian translation printed in Florence shortly after the Council adjourned. Before long, translations appeared also in Germany, South America, and even in Strossmayer's native land. An English translation was reported in the *Guardian* of June 28, 1871. It bore the title: "The speech of Bishop Strossmayer on the infallibility of the pope, delivered before the late Ecumenical Council in Rome." Even today the speech continues to be distributed under Strossmayer's name. It was published as recently as 1967 in Belgrade, Yugoslavia, in a book containing a selection of famous speeches. Evidently, while the content reveals familiarity with the leading personalities at the Council, and with the arguments both pro and con, its genuineness is open to question. According to one writer, the real author was an obscure Mexican friar named José Augustin de Escudero.[12]

This dispute over authorship has had the negative effect of discrediting the contents and value of the tract itself. As was mentioned in earlier pages, forged documents played a significant part, not only in the development of papal power but also in the arguments used by the supporters of papal infallibility.[13]

---

11. James Hennesey, S. J., *The First Council of the Vatican*, 1963, 184.

12. Dr. Adrian Fortescue, "A Slav Bishop, Joseph George Strossmayer," *Dublin Review*, October 1918, 251.

13. Hans Küng, *The Church*, 1967, 467, 488. See also Hasler, *How the Pope Became Infallible*, 176.

But most of these forgeries were palmed off as authoritative legal documents. If this tract be a forgery it does not fall into this category. It was simply a series of arguments, not based on questions of expediency or inexpediency, but on the main question of whether or not the doctrine of papal infallibility could stand the critical test of history and Scripture. It is with this in mind that the tract is included in this appendix.

An English translation of the Italian text of a speech published at Florence in 1870 under the name of Bishop Joseph Strossmayer

Venerable fathers and brethren – It is not without trembling, yet with a conscience free and tranquil before God who lives and sees me, that I open my mouth in the midst of you in this august assembly. From the time that I have been sitting here with you, I have followed with attention the speeches that have been made in the hall, hoping with great desire that a ray of light descending from on high might enlighten the eyes of my understanding, and permit me to vote the canons of this holy ecumenical Council with perfect knowledge of the case.

Holy Scripture and Papal Infallibility

Penetrated with the feelings of responsibility, of which God will demand of me an account, I have set myself to study with the most serious attention the Old and New Testaments, and I have asked these venerable monuments of truth to make known to me if the holy pontiff, who presides here, is truly the successor of St. Peter, vicar of Jesus Christ, and the infallible doctor of the Church. To resolve this grave question, I have been obliged to ignore the present state of things, and to transport myself in mind, with the evangelical torch in my hand, to the days when there was neither Ultramontanism nor Gallicanism, and in which the Church had for doctors St. Paul, St. Peter, St. James, and St. John – doctors to whom no one can deny the divine authority without putting in doubt that which the holy Bible, which is here before me, teaches us, and which the Council of Trent has proclaimed as the rule of faith and of morals. I have then opened these sacred pages. Well (shall I dare to say it?), I have found nothing either near nor far which sanctions the opinion of the Ultramontanes. And still more, to my very great surprise, I find in the apostolic days no question of a pope, successor to St. Peter, and vicar of Jesus Christ, any more than of Mahomet, who did not then exist. You, Monsignor Manning, will say that I blaspheme; You, Monsignor Fie, that I am mad. No, Monsignori, I do not blaspheme, and I am not mad. Now, having read the whole New Testament, I declare before God, with my hand raised to that great crucifix, that I have found no trace of the papacy as it exists at this moment. Do not refuse me your attention, my venerable brethren, and with your murmuring and interruptions do not justify those who say, like Father Hyacinthe, that this Council is nothing, but that our votes have been from the beginning dictated by authority. If such were the case, this august assembly, on which the eyes of the whole world are turned, would fall into the most shameful discredit. If we wish to make it great, we must be free. I thank his Excellency, Monsignor Dupanloup, for the sign of approbation he makes with his head: This gives me courage, and I go on.

Reading then the sacred books with the attention with which the Lord has made me capable, I do not find one single chapter, or one little verse, in which Jesus Christ gives to St. Peter the mastery over the apostles, his fellow workers. If Simon, son of Jonas, had been what we believe his holiness Pius IX to be today, it is wonderful that he had not said to him, "When I have ascended to my Father, you should all obey Simon Peter as you obey Me. I establish him my vicar upon Earth."

Not only is Christ silent on this point, but so little does he think of giving a head to the church that when he promises to his apostles to judge the twelve tribes of Israel (*Matthew* 19:28), he promises them twelve thrones, one for each, without saying that among those thrones one shall be higher than the others – which shall belong to Peter. Certainly, if he had wished that it should be so, He would have said it. What do we conclude from this sentence? Logic tells us that Christ did not wish to make St. Peter the head of the apostolic college. When Christ sent the apostles to conquer the world, to all he gave the promise of the Holy Spirit. Permit me to repeat it: If he had wished to constitute Peter his vicar, he would have given him the chief command over his spiritual army. Christ – so says the Holy Scripture – forbade Peter and his colleagues to reign or to exercise lordship, or to have authority over the faithful, like the kings of the Gentiles (*Luke* 22:25). If St. Peter had been elected pope, Jesus would not have spoken thus; but according to our tradition, the papacy holds in its hands two swords, symbols of spiritual and temporal power.

One thing has surprised me very much. Turning it over in my mind, I said to myself, "If Peter had been elected pope, would his colleagues have been permitted to send him with St. John to Samaria to announce the Gospel of the Son of God?" What do you think, venerable brethren, if at this moment we permitted ourselves to send his Holiness Pius IX and his Excellency Monsignor Plantier to go to the Patriarch of Constantinople, to pledge him to put an end to the Eastern schism?

But here is another still more important fact. An ecumenical council is assembled at Jerusalem to decide on the questions that divide the faithful. Who would have called together this council if St. Peter had been pope? St. Peter. Who would have presided at it? St. Peter or his legate. Who would have promulgated the canons? St. Peter. Well, nothing of this occurred. The apostle assisted at the council as all the others did, yet it was not he who summed up, but St. James; and when the decrees were promulgated, it was in the name of the apostles, the elders, and the brethren (*Acts* 15). Is it thus that we do in our Church? The more I examine, O venerable brethren, the more I am convinced that in the Scriptures the son of Jonas does not appear to be first.

Now, while we teach that the Church is built upon St. Peter, St. Paul (whose authority cannot be doubted) says in his epistle to the *Ephesians* 2:20, it is built on the foundation of the apostles and prophets, Jesus Christ himself being the chief cornerstone. And the same apostle believes so little in the supremacy of St. Peter that he openly blames those who would say, "We are of Paul; we are of Apollos" (*1 Corinthians* 1:12), as those who say, "We are of Peter." If therefore this last apostle had been the Vicar of Christ, St. Paul would have taken great care not to censure so violently those who belonged to his own colleagues. The same apostle, counting up the offices of the church, mentions apostles, prophets, evangelists, doctors, and pastors. Is it to be believed, my venerable brethren, that St. Paul, the great apostle of the Gentiles, would have forgotten the first of these offices, the papacy, if the papacy had been of divine institution? The forgetfulness appeared to me to be as impossible as if an historian of this Council were not to mention one word of his holiness Pius IX. [Several voices – "Silence, heretic, silence."] Calm yourselves, my brethren, I have not yet finished. Forbidding me to go on, you show yourselves to the world to do wrong in shutting the mouth of the smallest member of this assembly.

I continue. The Apostle Paul makes no mention, in any of his letters directed to the various churches, of the primacy of Peter. If this primacy had existed, if, in one word, the church had in its body a supreme head infallible in teaching, would the great apostle of the Gentiles have forgotten to mention it? What do I say? He would have written a long letter on this all-important subject. Then, as he has actually done, when the edifice of the Christian doctrine is erected, would the foundation, the key of the arch, be forgotten? Now, unless you hold that the church of the apostles was heretical (which none of us would either desire or dare to say), we are obliged to confess that the church has never been more beautiful, more pure, or more holy, than in the days when there was no pope. [Cries of, "It is not true; it is not true."] Let not Monsignor di Laval say, "No," since if any of you, my venerable brethren, should dare to think that the Church which has today a pope for its head is more in the faith, more pure in its morals than the apostolic church, let him say it openly in the face of the universe, for this enclosure is the center from which our words fly from pole to pole.

I go on. Neither in the writings of St. Paul, St. John, nor St. James have I found a trace or germ of the papal power. St. Luke, the historian of the missionary labors of the apostles, is silent on this all-important point. The silence of these holy men, whose writings make part of the canon of the divinely inspired Scriptures, has appeared to me burdensome and impossible, if Peter had been pope, and as unjustifiable as if Thiers, writing the history of Napoleon Bonaparte, had omitted the title of Emperor.

I see here before me a member of the assembly, who says, pointing at me with his finger, "There is a schismatic Bishop who has got among us under false colors." No, no, my venerable brethren, I have not entered this august assembly as a thief, by the window, but by the door like yourselves. My title of Bishop gave me a right to it, as my Christian conscience forces me to speak and to say that which I believe to be true.

What has surprised me most, and what moreover is capable of demonstration, is the silence of St. Peter. If the apostle had been what we proclaim him to be – that is, the vicar of Jesus Christ on Earth – he surely would have known it; if he had known it, how is it that not once did he act as pope? He might have done it on the day of Pentecost, when he pronounced his first sermon, but did not do it; neither in the two letters directed to the church. Can you imagine such a pope, my venerable brethren, if St. Peter had been pope? Now, if you wish to maintain that he was the pope, the natural consequence arises that you must maintain that he was ignorant of the fact. Now I ask whoever has a head to think and a mind to reflect, are these two suppositions possible?

To return, I say, while the apostle lived, the church never thought that there could be a pope; to maintain the contrary, all the sacred writings must be entirely ignored.

Tradition and Legend

But it is said on all sides, "Was not St. Peter at Rome? Was he not crucified with his head down? Are not the pulpits in which he taught, the altars at which he said the mass, in this eternal city?" St. Peter having been at Rome, my venerable brethren, rests only on tradition; but, if he had been Bishop of Rome, how can you from that episcopate prove his supremacy? Scaliger, one of the most learned of men, has not hesitated to say that St. Peter's episcopate and residence at Rome ought to be classed with ridiculous legends. [Repeated cries, "Shut his mouth, shut his mouth; make him come down from the pulpit."]

Venerable brethren, I am ready to be silent; but is it not better, in an assembly like ours, to prove all things, as the apostle commands, and to hold fast what is good? We have a dictator, before whom we – even his holiness Pius IX himself – must prostrate ourselves, and be silent and bow our heads. That dictator is history. This is not like a legend, which can be made as the potter makes his clay, but is like a diamond that cuts on the glass what cannot be canceled. Till now I have only leant on her; and if I have found no trace of the papacy in the apostolic days, the fault is hers, not mine. Do you wish to put me into the position of one accused of falsehood? You may do it, if you can.

I hear from the right someone expressing these words: "You are Peter, and on this rock I will build my church." I will answer this objection presently, my venerable brethren; but, before doing so, I wish to present you with the result of my historical researches.

Finding no trace of the papacy in the days of the apostles, I said to myself, I shall find what I am in search of in the annals of the Church. Well, I say it frankly – I have sought for a pope in the first four centuries, and I have not found him. None of you, I hope, will doubt the great authority of the holy Bishop of Hippo, the great and blessed St. Augustine. This pious doctor – the honor and glory of the Catholic Church – was secretary in the Council of Melvie. In the decrees of this venerable assembly are to be found these significant words – "Whoever wills to appeal to those beyond the sea shall not be received by anyone in Africa to the communion." The Bishops of Africa acknowledged the Bishop of Rome so little that they smote with excommunication those who would have recourse to an appeal. These same Bishops, in the sixth Council of Carthage, held under Aurelius, Bishop of that city, wrote to Celestinus, Bishop of Rome, to warn him not to receive appeals from the Bishops, priests, or clerics of Africa; and that he should send no more legates or commissaries; and that he should not introduce human pride into the Church.

That the Patriarch of Rome had from the earliest times tried to draw to himself all authority is an evident fact; but it is an equally evident fact that he had not the supremacy, which the Ultramontanes attribute to him. Had he possessed it, would the bishops of Africa – St. Augustine first among them – have dared to prohibit the appeals of their decrees to his supreme tribunal? I confess without difficulty that the Patriarch of Rome held the first place. One of Justinian's laws says, "Let us order, after the definition of the four Councils, that the holy pope of ancient Rome shall be the first of the Bishops, and that the most high Archbishop of Constantinople, which is the new Rome, shall be the second." "Bow down then to the supremacy of the pope," you will say to me. Do not run so fast to this conclusion, my venerable brethren, inasmuch as the law of Justinian has written on the face of it, "Of the order of the patriarchal sees." Precedence is one thing; the power of jurisdiction is another. For example, supposing that in Florence there was an assembly of all the Bishops of the kingdom, the precedence would be given to the Primate of Florence, as among the Easterns it would be accorded to the Patriarch of Constantinople, as in England to the Archbishop of Canterbury. But neither the first, nor the second, nor the third could deduce from the position assigned to him a jurisdiction over his colleagues.

The importance of the Bishops of Rome proceeded not from a divine power, but from the importance of the city in which they had their seat. Monsignor Darboy (in Paris) is not superior in dignity to the Archbishop of Avignon; but, in spite of that, Paris gives him a consideration, which he would not have, if, instead of having his palace on the bank of the Seine, he had it on that of the Rhone. That which is true in the religious order is the same in civil and political matters: The Prefect of Rome is not more a prefect than one at Pisa; but civilly and politically he has a greater importance.

I have said that from the very first centuries the Patriarch of Rome aspired to the universal government of the church. Unfortunately he very nearly reached it; but he had not succeeded assuredly in his pretensions, for the Emperor Theodosius II made a law by which he established that the Patriarch of Constantinople should have the same authority as he of Rome (*Leg. cod. de sacr., etc.*). The fathers of the Council of Chalcedon put the Bishops of the new and the old Rome in the same order on all things, even ecclesiastical (*Canon* 28). The sixth Council of Carthage forbade all the Bishops to take the title of prince of the Bishops, or sovereign Bishop. As for this title of universal Bishop, which the popes took later, St. Gregory I, believing that his successors would never think of adorning themselves with it, wrote these remarkable words: "None of my predecessors has consented to take this profane name; for when a patriarch gives himself the name of *Universal*, the title of Patriarch suffers discredit. Far be it then from Christians to desire to give themselves a title which brings discredit upon their brethren!"

The words of St. Gregory are directed to his colleagues of Constantinople, who pretended to the primacy of the church. Pope Pelagius II calls John, Bishop of Constantinople, who aspired to the high priesthood, "impious and profane." "Do not care," he said, "for the title of universal, which John has usurped illegally. Let none of the patriarchs take this profane name; for what misfortunes may we not expect, if among the priests such elements arise? They would get what has been foretold for them – He is the king of the sons of pride" (Pelagius II, *Letter 13*). Do not these authorities prove (and I might add a hundred more of equal value), with a clearness as the Sun at midday, that the first Bishops of Rome were not till much later recognized as universal Bishops and heads of the church? And on the other hand, who does not know that from the year 325, in which the first Council of Nicea was held, down to 580, the year of the Second Ecumenical Council of Constantinople, among more than 1,109 Bishops who assisted at the first six general councils, there were not more than nineteen Western Bishops? Who does not know that the Emperors convoked the councils without informing, and sometimes against the wish of, the Bishop of Rome? – That Hosius, Bishop of Cordova, presided at the first Council of Nice, and edited the canons of it? The same Hosius presided afterward at the Council of Sardica, excluding the legates of Julius, Bishop of Rome.

The Petrine Fiction

I say no more, my venerable brethren; and I come now to speak of the great argument – which you mentioned before – to establish the primacy of the Bishop of Rome by the rock (*petra*). If this were true, the dispute would be at an end; but our forefathers – and they certainly knew something – did not think of it as we do. St. Cyril in his fourth book on the Trinity says, "I believe that by the rock you must understand the unshaken faith of the apostles." St. Hilary, Bishop of Poitiers, in his second book on the Trinity says, "The rock (*petra*) is the blessed and only rock of the faith confessed by the mouth of St. Peter," and in the sixth book of the Trinity he says, "It is on this rock of the confession of the faith that the church is built." "God," says St. Jerome in the sixth book on *St. Matthew*, "has founded his church on this rock, and it is from this rock that the apostle Peter has been named." After him St. Chrysostom says in his fifty-third homily on *St. Matthew*, "On this rock I will build my church – that is, on the faith of the confession." Now, what was the confession of the apostle? Here it is – "You are the Christ, the Son of the living God." Ambrose, the holy Archbishop of Milan (on the second chapter of the *Ephesians*), St. Basil of Seleucia, and the fathers of the Council of Chalcedon, teach exactly the same thing. Of all the doctors of Christian antiquity St. Augustine occupies one of the first places for knowledge and holiness. Listen then to what he writes in his second treatise on the *First Epistle of St. John*: "What do the words mean, 'I will build my church on this rock'? *On this faith*, on that which said, 'You are the Christ, the Son of the living God.'" In his treatise on *St. John* we find this most significant phrase: "On this rock which you have confessed I will build my church, since Christ was the rock." The great Bishop believed so little that the church was built on St. Peter that he said to the people in his thirteenth sermon, "You are Peter, and on this rock (*petra*) which you have confessed, on this rock which you have known, saying, 'You are Christ, the Son of the living God,' I will build my church – upon myself, who am the Son of the living God: I will build it on me, and not me on you." That which St. Augustine thought upon this celebrated passage was the opinion of all Christendom in his time.

Therefore, to resume, I establish: (1) That Jesus has given his apostles the same power that he gave to St. Peter. (2) That the apostles never recognized in St. Peter the vicar of Jesus Christ and the infallible doctor of the church. (3) That St. Peter never thought of being pope, and never acted as if he were pope. (4) That the councils of the first four centuries, while they recognized the high position which the Bishop of Rome occupied in the church on account of Rome, only accorded to him a pre-eminence of honor, never of power or of jurisdiction. (5) That the holy fathers in the famous passage, "You are Peter, and on this rock I will build my church," never understood that the church was built on Peter (*super Petrum*) but on the rock (*super petram*), that is, on the confession of the faith of the apostle. I conclude victoriously, with history, with reason, with logic, with good sense, and with a Christian conscience, that Jesus Christ did not confer any supremacy on St. Peter, and that the Bishops of Rome did not become sovereigns of the church, but only by confiscating one by one all the rights of the episcopate. [Voices – "Silence, impudent Protestant! Silence!"]

The Errors of the Popes

No, I am not an impudent Protestant. History is neither Catholic, nor Anglican, nor Calvinistic, nor Lutheran, nor Arminian, nor schismatic Greek nor Ultramontane. She is what she is – that is, something stronger than all confessions of faith or the canons of the ecumenical councils. Write against it, if you dare, but you cannot destroy it, any more than taking a brick out of the Coliseum would make it fall. If I have said anything which history proves to be false, show it to me by history, and without a moment's hesitation I will make an honorable apology; but be patient, and you will see that I have not said all that I would or could; and even were the funeral pyre waiting for me in the place of St. Peter's, I should not be kept silent, and I am obliged to go on. Monsignor Dupanloup, in his celebrated *Observations* on this Council of the Vatican, has said, and with reason, that if we declare Pius IX infallible, we must necessarily, and from natural logic, be obliged to hold that all his predecessors were also infallible.

Well, venerable brethren, here history raises its voice to assure us that some popes have erred. You may protest against it or deny it, as you please, but I will prove it. Pope Victor (189-199) first approved of Montanism, and then condemned it. Marcellinus (296-304) was an idolater. He entered into the temple of Vesta, and offered incense to the goddess. You will say that it was an act of weakness; but I answer, a vicar of Jesus Christ dies rather than become an apostate. Liberius (352-366) consented to the condemnation of Athanasius, and made a profession of Arianism, that he might be recalled from his exile and reinstated in his see. Honorius (625-638) adhered to Monothelitism: Father Gratry has proved it to demonstration. Gregory I (590-604) calls anyone Antichrist who takes the name of Universal Bishop; and contrariwise Boniface III (607-608) made the parricide Emperor Phocas confer that title upon him. Paschal II (1099-1118) and Eugene III (1145-1153) authorized dueling; Julius II (1503-13) and Pius IV (1559-1565) forbade it. Eugene IV (1431-1447) approved of the Council of Basle and the restitution of the chalice to the church of Bohemia; Pius II (1458-1464) revoked the concession. Adrian II (867-872) declared civil marriages to be valid; Pius VII (1800-1823) condemned them. Sixtus V (1585-1590) published an edition of the Bible, and by a bull recommended it to be read; Pius VII condemned the reading of it. Clement XI (1700-1721) abolished the order of the Jesuits, permitted by Paul III, and Pius VII reestablished it.

But why look for such remote proofs? Has not our holy father here present, in his bull that gave the rules for this Council, in the event of his dying while it was sitting, revoked all that in past times may be contrary to it, even when that proceeds from the decisions of his predecessors? And certainly, if Pius IX has spoken *ex cathedra*, it is not when from the depths of his sepulcher he imposes his will on the sovereigns of the church. I should never finish, my venerable brethren, if I were to put before your eyes the contradictions of the popes in their teaching. If then you proclaim the infallibility of the actual pope, you must declare that the Holy Spirit has revealed to you that the infallibility of the papacy dates only from 1870. Are you bold enough to do this?

Perhaps the people may be indifferent, and pass by theological questions which they do not understand, and of which they do not see the importance; but though they are indifferent to principles, they are not so to facts. Do not then deceive yourselves. If you decree the dogma of papal infallibility, the Protestants, our adversaries, will mount in the breach, the more bold that they have history on their side, whilst we have only our own denial against them. What can we say to them when they show up all the Bishops of Rome from the days of Luke to his Holiness Pius IX? Ah! If they had all been like Pius IX, we should triumph on the whole line; but, alas! it is not so. [Cries of "Silence, silence; enough, enough!"]

Do not cry out, Monsignori! To fear history is to own yourselves conquered and, moreover, if you made the whole waters of the Tiber pass over it, you would not cancel a single page. Let me speak, and I will be as short as it is possible on this most important subject. Pope Vigilius (537-555) purchased the papacy from Belisarius, lieutenant of the Emperor Justinian. It is true that he broke his promise and never paid for it. Is this a canonical mode of binding on the tiara? The second Council of Chalcedon had formally condemned it. In one of its canons you read "The Bishop who obtains his episcopate by money shall lose it and be degraded." Pope Eugene III [IV in original] (1145-1153) imitated Vigilius. St. Bernard, the bright star of his age, reproves the pope, saying to him, "Can you show me in this great city of Rome anyone who would receive you as pope if they had not received gold or silver for it?"

My venerable brethren, will a pope who establishes a bank at the gates of the temple be inspired by the Holy Spirit? Will he have any right to teach the church infallibly? You know the history of Formosus too well for me to add to it. Stephen XI caused his body to be exhumed, dressed in his pontifical robes; he made the fingers which he used for giving the benediction to be cut off, and then had him thrown into the Tiber, declaring him to be a perjurer and illegitimate. He was then imprisoned by the people, poisoned, and strangled. Look how matters were readjusted: Romanus, successor of Stephen, and after him John X, rehabilitated the memory of Formosus.

But you will tell me these are fables, not history. Fables! Go, Monsignori, to the Vatican library and read Platina, the historian of the papacy, and the annals of Baronius (A.D. 897).[14] These are facts, which, for the honor of the Holy See, we should wish to ignore; but when it is to define a dogma which may provoke a great schism in our midst, the love which we bear to our venerable mother church, catholic, apostolic, and Roman, ought it to impose silence on us?

I go on. The learned Cardinal Baronius, speaking of the papal court, says (give attention, my venerable brethren, to

14. Baronius (1538-1607) wrote the *Annales Ecclesiastici* from 1558-1607. The dates given in the text refer to years he discusses in his *Annales*. – Editor.

these words), "What did the Roman Church appear in those days? How infamous! Only all-powerful courtesans governing in Rome! It was they who gave, exchanged, and took bishoprics; and, horrible to relate, they got their lovers, the false popes, put on the throne of St. Peter" (Baronius, A.D. 912). You will answer, "These were false popes, not true ones." Let it be so; but in that case, if for fifty years the see of Rome was occupied by anti-popes, how will you pick up again the thread of pontifical succession? Has the Church been able, at least for a century and a half, to go on without a head, and find itself acephalous?

Look now: The greatest number of these anti-popes appear in a genealogical tree of the papacy; and it must have been this absurdity that Baronius described; because Genebrardo, the great flatterer of the popes, had dared to say in his *Chronicles*[15] (A.D. 901), "This century is unfortunate, as for nearly 150 years the popes have fallen from all the virtues of their predecessors and have become apostates rather than apostles." I can understand how the illustrious Baronius must have blushed when he narrated the acts of these Roman Bishops. Speaking of John XI (931-935), natural son of Pope Sergius and of Marozia, he wrote these words in his annals: "The holy church, that is, the Roman, has been vilely trampled on by such a monster." John XII (956-964), elected pope at the age of eighteen through the influence of courtesans, was not one whit better than his predecessor.

I grieve, my venerable brethren, to stir up so much filth. I am silent on Alexander VI, father and lover of Lucretia; I turn away from John XXII (1319), who denied the immortality of

15. Genebrardo wrote his *Chronicles* in 1567. The dates in the text refer to years he discusses in his *Chronicles*. – *Editor.*

the soul and was deposed by the holy Ecumenical Council of Constance. Some will maintain that this council was only a private one; let it be so; but if you refuse any authority to it, as a logical sequence you must hold the nomination of Martin V (1417-1431) to be illegal. What, then, will become of the papal succession? Can you find the thread of it?

I do not speak of the schisms that have dishonored the church. In those unfortunate days the see of Rome was occupied by two competitors, and sometimes even by three. Which of these was the true pope? Resuming once more, again I say, if you decree the infallibility of the present Bishop of Rome, you must establish the infallibility of all the preceding ones, without excluding any. But can you do that, when history is establishing with clearness equal to that of the Sun that the popes have erred in their teaching? Could you do it and maintain that avaricious, incestuous, murdering, simoniacal popes have been vicars of Jesus Christ? Oh, venerable brethren, to maintain such an enormity would be to betray Christ worse than Judas! It would be to throw dirt in his face. [Cries, "Down from the pulpit, quick; shut the mouth of the heretic!"]

My venerable brethren, you cry out; but would it not be more dignified to weigh my reasons and my proofs in the balance of the sanctuary? Believe me, history cannot be made over again; it is there, and will remain to all eternity, to protest energetically against the dogma of papal infallibility. You may proclaim it unanimously; but one vote will be wanting, and that is mine! Monsignori, the true and faithful have their eyes on us, expecting from us a remedy for the innumerable evils, which dishonor the church: Will you deceive them in their hopes? What will not our responsibility before God be, if we let this solemn occasion pass which God has given us to heal the true faith? Let us seize it, my brethren; let us arm ourselves with a holy courage; let us make a violent and generous effort; let us turn to the teaching of the apostles, since without that we have only errors, darkness, and false traditions. Let us avail ourselves of our reason and of our intelligence to take the apostles and prophets as our only infallible masters with reference to the question of questions: "What must I do to be saved?" When we have decided that, we shall have laid the foundation of our dogmatic system firm and immovable on the rock, lasting and incorruptible, of the divinely inspired Holy Scriptures. Full of confidence, we will go before the world and, like the apostle Paul, in the presence of the free-thinkers, we will "know none other than Jesus Christ, and him crucified." We will conquer through the preaching of "the folly of the cross," as Paul conquered the learned men of Greece and Rome; and the Roman Church will have its glorious '89. [Clamorous cries "Get down! Out with the Protestant, the Calvinist, the traitor of the church."] Your cries, Monsignori, do not frighten me. If my words are hot, my head is cool. I am neither of Luther, nor of Calvin, nor of Paul, nor of Apollos, but of Christ. [Renewed cries, "Anathema, anathema, to the apostate."]

Anathema? Monsignori, anathema? You know well that you are not protesting against me, but against the holy apostles under whose protection I should wish this Council to place the Church. Ah! If wrapped in their winding-sheets they came out of their tombs, would they speak a language different from mine? What would you say to them when by their writings they tell you that the papacy had deviated from the Gospel of the Son of God, which they have preached and confirmed in so generous a manner by their blood? Would you dare say to them, "We prefer the teaching of our own popes, our Bellarmine, our Ignatius Loyola, to yours?" No, no! A thousand times, no, unless you have shut your ears that you may not hear, closed your eyes that you may not see, blunted your mind that you may not understand. Ah! If he who reigns above wishes to punish us, making his hand fall heavy on us, as he did on Pharaoh, he has no need to permit Garibaldi's soldiers to drive us away from the eternal city. He has only to let them make Pius IX a god, as we have made a goddess of the blessed virgin. Stop, stop, venerable brethren, on the odious and ridiculous incline on which you have placed yourselves. Save the Church from the shipwreck that threatens her, asking from the Holy Scriptures alone for the rule of faith we ought to believe and to profess. I have spoken: May God help me![16]

16. Although Strossmayer withstood the pressure for three years, he was finally broken by the Vatican and assented to papal infallibilty. – *Editor*

The Donation of Constantine

As given in part one, division XCVI, chapters XIII and
XIV of Gratian's *Decretum,* or *Harmony of the Canons.*
PALEA[1]

CHAPTER XIII. CONCERNING THE SAME[2]

T HE Emperor Constantine yielded his crown and all
his royal prerogatives in the city of Rome, and in Italy,
and in western parts to the Apostolic [See]. For in the Acts
of the Blessed Sylvester (which the Blessed Pope Gelasius in
the Council of the Seventy Bishops recounts as read by the
catholic, and in accordance with ancient usage many churches
he says follow this example) occurs the following:

PALEA

CHAPTER XIV. CONCERNING THE SAME

The Emperor Constantine the fourth day after his baptism
conferred this privilege on the Pontiff of the Roman Church,

1. The meaning of this word in this connection is unknown. The chapters
to which it is prefixed are for the most part supposed to have been early
marginal annotations afterwards incorporated in the text of the *Decretum.*
See Friedberg, *Corpus Iuris canonici,* volume 1, Prolegomena, lxxxvi.

2. The subject of chapters xi and xii is, "The Emperors must be under
the Pontiffs, not over them." Chapters xiii and xiv continue the same
subject.

in the whole Roman world priests should regard him as their head, as judges do the king. In this privilege among other things is this: "We – together with all our satraps, and the whole senate and my nobles, and also all the people subject to the government of glorious Rome – considered it advisable, that as the Blessed Peter is seen to have been constituted vicar of the Son of God on the Earth, so the Pontiffs who are the representatives of that same chief of the apostles, should obtain from us and our Empire the power of a supremacy greater than the clemency of our earthly Imperial serenity is seen to have conceded to it, choosing that same chief of the apostles and his vicars to be our constant intercessors with God. And to the extent of our earthly Imperial power, we have decreed that his holy Roman Church shall be honored with veneration, and that more than our Empire and earthly throne the most sacred seat of the Blessed Peter shall be gloriously exalted, we giving to it power, and dignity of glory and vigor, and honor Imperial. And we ordain and decree that he shall have the supremacy as well over the four principal seats Alexandria, Antioch, Jerusalem, and Constantinople, as also over all the churches of God in the whole Earth. And Pontiff, who at the time shall be at the head of the holy Roman Church itself, shall be more exalted than, and chief over, all the priests of the whole world, and according to his judgment everything which is provided for the service of God and for the stability of the faith of Christians is to be administered. *And below:*

§1. On the churches of the blessed apostles Peter and Paul, for the providing of the lights, we have conferred landed estates of possessions, and have enriched them with different objects and through our sacred Imperial mandate we have granted him of our property in the east as well as in the west, and even in the northern and the southern quarter; namely, in Judea,

Greece, Asia, Thrace, Africa, and Italy and the various islands; under this condition indeed, that all shall be administered by the hand of our most blessed father the supreme Pontiff, Sylvester, and his successors. *And below:*

§2. And to our Father, the Blessed Sylvester, supreme Pontiff and Pope universal, of the city of Rome, and to all the Pontiffs, his successors, who shall sit in the seat of the Blessed Peter even unto the end of the world, we by this present do give our Imperial Lateran Palace, then the diadem, that is, the crown of our head, and at the same time the tiara and also the shoulder-band – that is, the strap that usually surrounds our Imperial neck; and also the purple mantle and scarlet tunic, and all the Imperial raiment; and also the same rank as those presiding over the Imperial cavalry conferring also even the Imperial scepters, and at the same time all the standards, and banners, and the different ornaments, and all the pomp of our Imperial eminence, and the glory of our power.

§3. We decree moreover, as to the most reverend men, the clergy of different orders who serve that same holy Roman Church, that they have that same eminence, distinction, power and excellence, by the glory of which it seems proper for our most illustrious senate to be adorned; that is, that they be made patricians and consuls, and also we have proclaimed that they be decorated with the other Imperial dignities. And even as the Imperial militia is adorned, so also we decree that the clergy of the holy Roman Church be adorned. And even as the Imperial power is adorned with different offices, of chamberlains, indeed, and door-keepers, and all the guards, so we wish the holy Roman Church also to be decorated. And in order that the pontifical glory may shine forth most fully, we decree this also; that the horses of the clergy of this same holy Roman Church be decorated with saddle-cloths and linens, that is of the whitest color, and that they are to so ride. And even as our senate uses shoes with felt socks, that is, distinguished by white linen, so the clergy also should use them, so that, even as the celestial orders, so also the terrestrial may be adorned to the glory of God.

§4. Above all things, moreover, we give permission to that same most holy one our Father Sylvester and to his successors, from our edict, that he may make priest whomever he wishes, according to his own pleasure and counsel, and enroll him in the number of the religious clergy [*i.e.*, regular, or monastic, clergy; or, perhaps, the cardinals], let no one whomsoever presume to act in a domineering way in this.

§5. We also therefore decreed this, that he himself and his successors might use and bear upon their heads – to the praise of God for the honor of the Blessed Peter – the diadem, that is, the crown which we have granted him from our own head, of purest gold and precious gems. But since he himself, the most blessed Pope, did not at all allow that crown of gold to be used over the clerical crown which he wears to the glory of the Blessed Peter, we placed upon his most holy head, with our own hands, a glittering tiara of dazzling white representing the Lord's resurrection, and holding the bridle of his horse, out of reverence for the Blessed Peter, we performed for him the duty of groom, decreeing that all his successors and they alone, use this same tiara in processions in imitation of our power.

§6. Wherefore, in order that the supreme pontificate may not deteriorate, but may rather be adorned with glory and power even more than is the dignity of an earthly rule; behold, we give over and relinquish to the aforesaid our most blessed Pontiff, Sylvester, the universal Pope, as well our palace, as has been said, as also the city of Rome, and all the provinces, places and cities of Italy and the western regions, and we decree by this our godlike and pragmatic sanction that they are to be controlled by him and by his successors, and we grant that they shall remain under the law of the holy Roman Church.

§7. Wherefore we have perceived it to be fitting that our Empire and the power of our kingdom should be transferred in the regions of the East, and that in the province of Byzantia, in the most fitting place, a city should be built in our name, and that our Empire should there be established, for where the supremacy of priests and the head of the Christian religion has been established by the heavenly Emperor, it is not right that there an earthly Emperor should have jurisdiction.

§8. We decree, moreover, that all these things, which through this our sacred Imperial [charter] through other godlike decrees we have established and confirmed, remain inviolate and unshaken unto the end of the world. Wherefore, before the living God who commanded us to reign, and in the face of his terrible judgment, we entreat, through this our Imperial sanction, all the Emperors our successors, and all the nobles, the satraps also, the most glorious senate, and all the people in the whole world, now and in all times still[3] to come subject to our rule, that no one of them in any way be allowed either to break these [decrees], or in any way overthrow them. If any one, moreover – which we do not believe – prove a scorner or despiser in this matter, he shall be subject and bound over to eternal damnation, and shall feel the holy ones of God, the chief of the apostles, Peter and Paul, opposed to him in the present and in the future life, and he shall be burned in the lower Hell and shall perish with the devil and all the impious.

---

3. *Retro* was used at Rome in the latter part of the eighth century with the peculiar meaning of "still" or "again." This is one of the clues to the date and place of the document. Henderson's translation is erroneous.

The page, moreover, of this our Imperial decree, we, confirming it with our own hands, did place above the venerable body of the Blessed Peter, chief of the apostles. Given at Rome on the third day before the Kalends of April, our master the august Flavius Constantine, for the fourth time, and Gallicanus, most illustrious men, being consuls.

Glossary

Bishop – In the Roman Catholic Church, the title of an ecclesiastical dignitary who possesses the fullness of the priesthood to rule a diocese as its chief pastor, in due submission to the primacy of the pope. It is of the Catholic faith that Bishops are of divine institution. In the hierarchy of order they possess powers superior to those of priests and deacons; in the hierarchy of jurisdiction, by Christ's will, they are appointed for the government of one portion of the faithful of the Church, under the direction and authority of the sovereign pontiff, who can determine and restrain their powers, but not annihilate them. They are the successors of the apostles, though they do not possess all the prerogatives of the latter. The episcopate is monarchical. By the will of Christ, the supreme authority in a diocese does not belong to a college of priests or of Bishops, but it resides in the single personality of the chief. The Bishop is the highest of three ordained offices in the Roman Church: deacon, priest, Bishop.

Bull – A *bulla* was originally a circular plate or boss of metal, so called from its resemblance in form to a bubble floating upon water (Latin *bullire*, to boil). In the course of time the term came to be applied to the leaden seals with which papal and royal documents were authenticated in the early Middle Ages, and by a further development, the name, from designating the seal, was eventually attached to the document itself. This did not happen before the thirteenth century and the name *bull* was only a popular term used almost promiscuously for all kinds of instruments, which issued from the papal chancery. A much more precise acceptance has prevailed since the fifteenth century, and a bull has long stood in sharp contrast with certain other forms of papal documents. For practical purposes a bull may be conveniently defined to be "an apostolic letter with a leaden seal," to which one may add that in its superscription the pope invariably takes the title of *episcopus, servus servorum Dei.*

Canon Law – Canon Law is the body of laws and regulations made by or adopted by ecclesiastical authority for the government of the Roman Church and its members. The word *adopted* is here used to point out the fact that there are certain elements in Canon Law borrowed by the Church from civil law or from the writings of private individuals, who as such had no authority in ecclesiastical society. The expression "canon law" (*jus canonicum*) became current only about the beginning of the twelfth century, being used in contrast with the "civil law" (*jus civile*), and later we have the "Corpus juris canonici," as we have the "Corpus juris civilis." Canon Law is also called "ecclesiastical law" (*jus ecclesiasticum*); however, strictly speaking, there is a slight difference of meaning between the two expressions: Canon law denotes in particular the law of the "Corpus Juris," including the regulations borrowed from Roman law; whereas ecclesiastical law refers to all laws made by the ecclesiastical authorities as such, including those made after the compiling of the "Corpus Juris." Contrasted with the imperial or Caesarian law (*jus caesareum*), Canon Law is sometimes styled pontifical law (*jus pontificium*), often also it is termed sacred law (*jus sacrum*), and sometimes even Divine law (*jus divinum*: c. 2, De privil.), as it concerns holy things, and has for its object the well-being of souls.

Cardinal – A dignitary of the Roman Church and counsellor of the pope. A Cardinal may be a Bishop, a priest, or a deacon.

Decretal – In the wide sense of the term, *decretalis* (*i.e. epistola decretalis*) signifies a pontifical letter containing a *decretum*, or pontifical decision. In a narrower sense it denotes a decision on a matter of discipline. In the strictest sense of the word, it means a rescript (*rescriptum*), *i.e.,* an answer of the pope when he has been appealed to or his advice has been sought on a matter of discipline. Papal decretals, therefore, are not necessarily general laws of the Church. But frequently the pope ordered the recipient of his letter to communicate the papal answer to the ecclesiastical authorities of the district to which he belonged; and it was their duty then to act in conformity with that decree when analogous cases arose. It is generally stated that the most ancient decretal is the letter of Pope Siricius (384-399) to Himerius, Bishop of Tarragona in Spain, dating from 385; but it would seem that the document of the fourth century known as "Canones Romanorum ad Gallos episcopos" is nothing else than an *epistola decretalis* of his predecessor, Pope Damasus (366-384), addressed to the bishops of Gaul. The decretals ought to be carefully distinguished from the canons of the councils; from the *epistol dogmatic, i.e.,* the pontifical documents touching on Catholic doctrine; from the *constitutiones,* or pontifical documents given *motu proprio,* that is, documents issued by the pope without his being asked to do so or consulted upon a subject.

Diet – In politics, a diet is a formal deliberative assembly. The term is derived from Medieval Latin *dietas*, and ultimately comes from the Latin *dies*, "day." The word came to be used in this sense because these assemblies met on a daily basis.

Encyclical – According to its etymology, an encyclical (from the Greek *egkyklios, kyklos* meaning a circle) is nothing more than a circular letter. In modern times, usage has confined the term almost exclusively to certain papal documents which differ in their technical form from the ordinary style of either Bulls or Briefs, and which in their superscription are explicitly addressed to the patriarchs, primates, archbishops, and bishops of the Catholic Church in communion with the apostolic see. By exception, encyclicals are also sometimes addressed to the archbishops and bishops of a particular country. Thus this name is given to the letter of Pius X (January 6, 1907) to the Bishops of France, in spite of the fact that it was published, not in Latin, but in French; while, on the other hand, the letter "Longinqua Oceani" (January 5, 1895) addressed by Leo XIII to the archbishops and bishops of the United States, is not styled an encyclical, although in all other respects it exactly observes the forms of one. From this and a number of similar facts we may probably infer that the precise designation used is not intended to be of any great significance. From the nature of the case encyclicals addressed to the bishops of the world are generally concerned with matters that affect the welfare of the Church at large. They condemn some prevalent form of error, point out dangers, which threaten faith or morals, exhort the faithful to constancy, or prescribe remedies for evils foreseen or already existent.

Legate – Legate, in its broad signification, means that person who is sent by another for some representative office. In the ecclesiastical sense it means one whom the pope sends to sovereigns or governments or only to the members of the episcopate and faithful of a country, as his representative, to treat of church matters or even on a mission of honor. Hence the legate differs from the delegate, taking this term in a strictly juridical sense, since the delegate is one to whom the pope entrusts an affair or many affairs to be treated through delegated jurisdiction and often in questions of litigation, whereas the legate goes with ordinary jurisdiction over a whole country or nation. The Canon Law treats of delegates of the Holy See, *delegati Sedis Apostolicæ*, and in this sense even Bishops, in certain cases determined by the Council of Trent, may act as delegates of the Holy See. Nevertheless, according to the present discipline of the Church, a delegate, inasmuch as he is sent to represent the Holy See in some particular country, really fills the office of a legate. Since the jurisdiction of a legate is ordinary, he does not cease to be legate even at the death of the pope who appointed him, and even if he arrived at his post after the death of that pope.

Metropolitan – *Metropolitan,* in ecclesiastical language, refers to whatever relates to the metropolis, the principal city, or see, of an ecclesiastical province; thus we speak of a metropolitan church, a metropolitan chapter, a metropolitan official, etc. The word *metropolitan* used without any qualificative means the Bishop of the metropolitan see, now usually styled *archbishop.* The term metropolite (*Metropolites,* Metropolita) is also employed, especially in the Eastern Churches. The entire body of rights and duties which Canon Law attributes to the metropolitan, or archbishop as such, *i.e.,* not for his own diocese,

189

but for those suffragan to him and forming his ecclesiastical province, is called the *metropoliticum*.

Mitre – The mitre is a kind of folding-cap. It consists of two like parts, each stiffened by a lining and rising to a peak; these are sewn together on the sides, but are united above by a piece of material that can fold together. Two lappets trimmed on the ends with fringe hang down from the back. The mitre is, theoretically, always supposed to be white. The pontifical mitre is of Roman origin; it is derived from a non-liturgical head-covering distinctive of the pope, the *camelaucum*, to which also the tiara is to be traced. The *camelaucum* was worn as early as the beginning of the eighth century, as is shown by the biography of Pope Constantine I (708-715) in the "Liber Pontificalis." The same headcovering is also mentioned in the so-called "Donation of Constantine." The Ninth Ordo states that the *camelaucum* was made of white stuff and shaped like a helmet. The coins of Sergius III (904-911) and of Benedict VII (974-983), on which St. Peter is portrayed wearing a *camelaucum*, give the cap the form of a cone, the original shape of the mitre. The *camelaucum* was worn by the pope principally during solemn processions. The mitre developed from the *camelaucum* in this way: In the course of the tenth century the pope began to wear this head-covering not merely during processions to the church, but also during the subsequent church service. Whether any influence was exerted by the recollection of the sacerdotal head-ornament of the high-priest of the Old Testament is not known, but probably not – at least there is no trace of any such influence. It was not until the mitre was universally worn by bishops that it was called an imitation of the Jewish sacerdotal head-ornament.

Pallium – The modern pallium is a circular band about two inches wide, worn about the neck, breast, and shoulders, and having two pendants, one hanging down in front and one behind. The pendants are about two inches wide and twelve inches long, and are weighted with small pieces of lead covered with black silk. The remainder of the pallium is made of white wool, part of which is supplied by two lambs presented annually as a tax by the Lateran Canons Regular to the Chapter of St. John on the feast of St. Agnes, solemnly blessed on the high altar of that church after the pontifical mass, and then offered to the pope. The ornamentation of the pallium consists of six small black crosses – one each on the breast and back, one on each shoulder, and one on each pendant. The crosses on the breast, back, and left shoulder are provided with a loop for the reception of a gold pin set with a precious stone. The pallium is worn over the chasuble.

Pontifex Maximus – The head priest of the Roman State religion was the Pontifex Maximus, or the greatest of the college of pontifices. While an obviously important and prominent position within the ranks of the Roman system, the Pontifex Maximus was not considered a magistrate comparable to a Consul, Praetor, etc. During the Republic, the Pontifex was elected by the Comitia Tributa and served for life, while during the Empire the position was generally held by the Emperor himself. By the Imperial period there were 16 pontifices under the high priest, 15 flamines, who were special priests of the main deities, and the Rex Sacrorum (king of the sacrifices) who performed the religious acts that the king had usually done. Interpreting omens, sometimes through auguries, controlling and keeping the official calendar, and the oversight of funerals all fell under the domain of the Pontifex Maximus. He was responsible for an enormous collection of omens (*annales maximi*); that would be recorded and collected on a nearly constant basis. These heavenly signs would be written down along with accompanying events, and used to determine the divine favor of the gods. Doing so allowed following generations of priests and magistrates to understand the historic will of the gods and interpret future events against past patterns. Today, the head of the Roman Catholic Church, the pope, is still called the Pontifex Maximus. It's a political or governing office that has been in existence and in perpetual use for nearly 3,000 years. It means the highest or greatest bridge between Heaven and Earth.

Pontiff – Pontiffs were originally simply chiefs or high priests of any religion; thus writers from the 16th through the 18th Centuries referred equally to Christian pontiffs (bishops) and "Mahometan [Muslim] Pontiffs" (caliphs). Over time, however, the term became associated with the highest religious authority in the Coptic and Catholic Churches – the pope. It was often modified by an adjective – for instance, "Alexandrian Pontiff," "Sovereign Pontiff," or "Roman Pontiff" – to distinguish from different pontiffs. In the modern era, the modifying adjective is usually dropped, with the term being used exclusively to refer to the Popes. *Pontiff* is derived from the Latin for bridge, *pons*.

See – From the Latin *Sancta Sedes*, Holy Chair. A term derived from the enthronement-ceremony of the Bishops of Rome. The seat or chair in question must not be confounded with the ancient *sedes gestatoria* in the center of the apse of St. Peter's, and immemorially venerated as the *cathedra Petri*, or Chair of Peter; the term means, in a general sense, the actual seat (*i.e.*, residence) of the supreme pastor of the Church, together with the various ecclesiastical authorities who constitute the central administration.

Ultramontanism – Literally, beyond the mountains. It is the term used to denote that faction within the Roman Church-State that advocated an absolute papal dictatorship.

Vincentian Rule – The Reformers and Anglican divines often quoted Vincent in their controversy with Rome. In his disputation at Oxford, Ridley said, when doubts arose in the Church, "I use the wise counsel of Vincentius Lirinensis, whom I am sure you will allow; who, giving precepts how the Catholic Church may be, in all schisms and heresies, known, writes on this manner: "When," he says, 'one part is corrupted with heresies then prefer the whole world before the one part: but if the greatest part be infected then prefer antiquity.'" Wherein it is also necessary to follow the universality, antiquity, and consent of the Catholic and Apostolic Church." This rule, which was so applauded by our Reformers as a guide for Catholics, is sometimes misunderstood and misapplied. Vincent sought to help those who were Catholics, and who believed in the Church as the organ through which Christ and the Holy Spirit spoke, to know what the Church had said. If there were seemingly conflicting voices, then by an appeal to universality, antiquity, and consent, to discern which was the authoritative and true one.

Bibliography

Alighieri, Dante. *La Divina Commedia.* Milano: Tipografia Editoriale Lucchi, 1959.

Atkinson, James. *The Trial of Luther.* London: B. T. Batsford, 1971.

Bainton, Roland H. *Early and Medieval Christianity.* Boston: The Beacon Press, 1962.

Bainton, Roland H. *The Reformation of the Sixteenth Century.* Boston: The Beacon Press, 1952.

Barnes, Alfred. *An Explanatory and Practical Commentary on Matthew.*

Barraclough, Geoffrey. *The Medieval Papacy.* London: Thames and Hudson, 1979.

Barzini, Luigi. *The Italians.* London: Hamish Hamilton, 1965.

Bettenson, Henry. *Documents of the Christian Church.* London: Oxford University Press, 1947.

Boettner, Loraine. *The Reformed Doctrine of Predestination.* Philadelphia: Presbyterian and Reformed Publishing Company, 1974.

Boettner, Loraine. *Roman Catholicism.* Philadelphia: Presbyterian and Reformed Publishing Company, 1962.

Brunner, Emil. *The Misunderstanding of the Church.* Translated by Harold Knight. London: Lutterworth Press, 1952.

Bury, J. B. *History of the Papacy in the 19th Century (1864-1878)*. London: Macmillan and Company, 1930.

Cantor, Norman F. *Medieval History, the Life and Death of a Civilization*. New York: Macmillan Company, 1964.

Carlyle, R. W. and A. J. *A History of Medieval Political Theory in the West*. 6 volumes. New York: Barnes and Noble, n.d.

Carnell, Edward John. *The Case for Biblical Christianity*. Edited by Ronald H. Nash. Grand Rapids: William B. Eerdmans, 1969.

Chadwick, Owen. *The Reformation*. Baltimore: Penguin Books, 1966.

Corbett, James A. *The Papacy, A Brief History*. New York: D. Van Nostrand Company, 1956.

D'Ormesson, Wladimir. *The Papacy*. Translated by Michael Derrick. Volume 81 of the *Twentieth Century Encyclopedia of Catholicism*. Edited by Henri Daniel Rops. New York: Hawthorne Books, 1959.

Dahmus, Joseph H. *A History of Medieval Civilization*. New York: The Odyssey Press, 1964.

Dalberg-Acton, John Emerich Edward. *The History of Freedom and Other Essays*. New York: Books for Libraries Press, 1967.

Daniel-Rops, Henri. *Cathedral and Crusade*. London: J. M. Dent and Sons, 1957.

Davis, John D. *The Westminster Dictionary of the Bible*.

Dawson, Christopher Henry. *The Dividing of Christendom*. New York: Sheed and Ward, 1965.

De Tocqueville, Alexis. *Democracy in America*. 2 volumes. New York, 1945.

Defensorium Obedientiae Apostolicae Et Alia Documenta. Translated and edited by Heiko A. Oberman, Daniel E. Zerfoss, and William J. Courtenay. Cambridge: The Belknap Press of Harvard University, 1968.

Denzinger, Henry. *Enchiridion Symbolorum, The Sources of Catholic Dogma.* Translated by Roy J. Deferrari. St. Louis: B. Herder Book Company, 1957.

Documents of Vatican II, The. Edited by Walter M. Abbott, S.J. New York: Herder and Herder, 1966.

Dolan, Thomas S. *The See of Peter and the Voice of Antiquity.* St. Louis: B. Herder, 1908.

Early Christian Fathers. Edited and translated by Cyril C. Richardson. Philadelphia: The Westminster Press, n.d.

Febvre, Lucien. *Martin Luther: A Destiny.* New York: E. P. Dutton and Company, 1929.

Flick, Alexander Clarence. *The Decline of the Medieval Church.* 2 volumes. New York: Alfred A. Knopp, 1930.

Gibbon, Edward. *The History of the Decline and Fall of the Roman Empire.* London: Ward, Lock and Company, n.d.

Gibbons, James Cardinal. *A Retrospect of Fifty Years.* 2 volumes. Baltimore: James Murphy Company, 1916.

Gieseler, John C. L. *A Text-Book of Church History.* Translated by Henry B. Smith. 5 volumes. New York: Harper & Brothers, 1876.

Giles, E. *Documents Illustrating Papal Authority* A.D. 96-454. London: SPCK, 1952.

Gilson, Etienne. *Reason and Revelation in the Middle Ages.* New York: Charles Scribner's Sons, 1938.

Gladstone, W. E. *Rome and the Newest Fashions in Religion.* London: John Murray, 1875.

Green, Samuel G. *A Handbook of Church History.* London: The Religious Tract Society, 1904.

Guicciardini, Francesco. *The History of Italy.* Translated by Sidney Alexander. New York: Macmillan Company, 1964.

Guillemain, Bernard. *The Later Middle Ages.* Translated by S. Taylor. Volume. 77 of the *Twentieth Century Encyclopedia of Catholicism.* Edited by Henri Daniel-Rops. New York: Hawthorne Books, 1959.

Hasler, August Bernhard. *How the Pope Became Infallible.* New York: Doubleday and Company, 1981.

Hastings, James. *Dictionary of the Bible.*

Headley, John M. *Luther's View of Church History.* New Haven: Yale University Press, 1963.

Hennesey, S. J., James. *The First Council of the Vatican.* New York: Herder and Herder, 1963.

Hillerbrand, Hans J. *The Reformation.* New York: Harper and Row, 1964.

Himmelfarb, Gertrude. *Lord Acton, A Study in Conscience and Politics.* Chicago: University of Chicago Press, 1952.

Hobbes, Thomas. *Leviathan.* New York: E. P. Dutton and Company, 1950.

Hughes, Philip. *A History of the Church.* 3 volumes. New York: Sheed and Ward, 1947.

Hyma, Albert. *Luther's Theological Development from Erfurt to Augsburg.* New York: F. S. Crofts and Company, 1928.

Hyma, Albert. *New Light on Martin Luther.* Grand Rapids: William B. Eerdmans Publishing Company, 1958.

Inside View of the Vatican Council, An. Edited by Leonard Woolsey Bacon. New York: American Tract Society, n.d.

Jacobs, Henry Eyster. *Martin Luther, the Hero of the Reformation, 1483-1546.* New York: G. P. Putnam's Sons, 1898.

Jalland, Trevor Gervase. *The Church and the Papacy.* London: SPCK, 1944.

Jedin, Hubert. *A History of the Council of Trent.* Translated by Ernest Graf. St. Louis: B. Herder Book Company, 1957.

Kidd, Dr. *Documents Illustrative of the History of the Church.* Volume 1, No. 74. London: SPCK, n.d.

Kittler, Glen D. *The Papal Princes.* New York: Funk & Wagnalls, 1960.

Küng, Hans. *The Church.* New York: Sheed and Ward, 1967.

Küng, Hans. *Infallible? An Enquiry.* Translated by Erich Mosbacher. London: William Collins Sons & Company, 1972.

Lightfoot, J. B. *The Apostolic Fathers.* London: Macmillan Company, 1890.

Lightfoot, John. *Hebrew and Talmudical Exercitations.* London: Oxford University Press, 1859.

Lucas, Henry S. *The Renaissance and the Reformation.* New York: Harper and Brothers, 1934.

Luther's Works. Jaroslav Pelikan and Helmut T. Lehmann, editors. 55 volumes. St. Louis: Concordia Publishing House and Muhlenburg Press, 1955.

MacDougal, H. A. *Lord Acton on Papal Power.* London: Sheed and Ward, 1973.

MacGregor, Geddes. *Corpus Christi, the Nature of the Church According to the Reformed Tradition.* Philadelphia: The Westminster Press, 1958.

MacGregor, Geddes. *The Vatican Revolution.* London: Macmillan and Company, 1958.

Mansi, Joannes Dominicus. *Sacrorum Conciliorun Nova et Aniplissima Collectio.* Graz: Akademishe Druck B U. Verlagsanstalt, 1961.

Martin Luthers Werke. Kritische Gesamtausgabe. Volumes 1 - , Weimar, 1853 -

McBrien, Richard P. *Catholicism.* 2 volumes. Minneapolis: Winston Press, 1980.

Neander, Augustus. *General History of the Christian Religion and Church.* Translated by Joseph Torrey. 10 volumes. London: Henry G. Bohn, 1851.

Nielsen, Fredrik. *The History of the Papacy in the XIXth Century.* 2 volumes. Translated by Arthur James Mason. London: John Murray, 1906.

Oberman, Heiko A. *The Harvest of Medieval Theology.* Cambridge: Harvard University Press, 1963.

Pelikan, Jaroslav. *Obedient Rebels.* New York: Harper and Row, 1964.

Pelikan, Jaroslav. *The Riddle of Roman Catholicism.* New York: Abingdon Press, 1959.

Pettingil, William L. *The Gospel of the Kingdom.*

Pinomaa, Lennart. *Faith Victorious.* Translated by Walter J. Kukkonen. Philadelphia: Fortress Press, 1963.

Plummer, Alfred. *An Exegetical Commentary of the Gospel of Matthew.*

Pope Paul VI. *Ecclesiam Suam.* Boston: Vatican Translation, Daughters of St. Paul, n.d.

Putnam, George Haven. *The Censorship of the Church of Rome.* 2 volumes. New York: G. P. Putman's Sons, 1907.

Readings in Church History. Edited by Colman J. Barry. 2 volumes. Westminster, Maryland: The Newman Press, 1960.

Robertson, A. T. *A Grammar of the Greek New Testament.* New York: Hodder & Stoughton, 1915.

Robertson, Alexander. *The Roman Catholic Church in Italy.* London: Morgan and Scott, 1904.

Rogers, C. F. *Rome and the Early Church.* London: SPCK, n.d.

Rupp, Gordon. *The Righteousness of God.* New York: Philosophical Library, 1953.

Salmon, George. *The Infallibility of the Church.* London: John Murray, 1914.

Schaff, Philip. *History of the Christian Church.* Associated Publishers and Authors, n.d.

Schulte, John. *Roman Catholicism, Old and New, from the Standpoint of the Infallibility Doctrine.* Toronto: Belford Brothers, 1876.

Schwiebert, E. G. *Luther and His Times.* St. Louis: Concordia Publishing House, 1950.

Smith, Preserved. *The Age of the Reformation.* New York: Henry Holt and Company, 1930.

Smith, Preserved. *The Life and Letters of Martin Luther.* New York: Houghton Mifflin Company, 1911.

Smith, William. *Dictionary of the Bible.* 4 volumes. Boston: Houghton, Mifflin and Company, 1870.

Tawney, R. H. *Religion and the Rise of Capitalism.* New York: New American Library, 1963.

Tierney, Brian. *The Crisis of Church and State.* Englewood Cliffs: Prentice-Hall, 1964.

Tierney, Brian. *Foundations of the Conciliar Theory.* Cambridge: Cambridge University Press, 1955.

Troeltsch, Ernst, *The Social Teaching of the Christian Churches.* Translated by Olive Wyon. Two Volumes. London: George Allen and Unwin, 1956.

Ullmann, Walter. *The Growth of Papal Government in the Middle Ages.* New York: Books for Libraries Press, 1967.

Ullmann, Walter. *Medieval Papalism, the Political Theories of the Medieval Canonists.* London: Methuen and Company, 1949.

Ullmann, Walter. *A Short History of the Papacy in the Middle Ages.* London: Methuen and Company, 1972.

Vincent, Marvin R. *Word Studies in the New Testament.*

Walker, C. S. M. *The Gathering Storm.* Grand Rapids: William B. Eerdmans Company, 1961.

Watson, Philip. *Let God be God.* Philadelphia: Fortress Press, 1947.

Weber, Max. *The Protestant Ethic and the Spirit of Capitalism.* Translated by Talcott Parsons.   London: Allen & Unwin, 1930.

Williams, Charles B. *The New Testament, A Translation in the Language of the People.* Chicago: Moody Press, 1950.

Works of Martin Luther. 6 volumes. Philadelphia: A. J. Holman Company, 1915-1932.

Scripture Index

Index

intellectual suicide 152
intrigues 151
invisible fellowship 85
invocation of saints 111
Iran 21
Irenaeus 44-45
irreformability 119
Israel 139, 162
Italian Renaissance 36
Italians, The (Barzini) 17-18, 25
Italy 13, 16-19, 22, 51, 107, 179,
181-182
"Iustitia Christi, and Iustitia Dei,
Luther and the Scholastic Doc-
trines of Justification" (Ober-
man) 92

Jacobs, Henry Eyster 86; *Works:
Martin Luther, The Hero of the
Reformation, 1483-1546* 86
Jalland, Trevor Gervase 72, 111,
121; *Works: The Church and the
Papacy* 72, 111, 121
James 136, 161, 163-164
Jansen, Cornelius Otto 113;
Works: Augustinus 113
Jansenism 113
Jedin, Hubert 77, 87, 106; *Works:
A History of the Council of Trent*
77, 106
Jerome 100, 170
Jerusalem 27, 135-136, 148, 163, 180
Jesuits 113, 151
Jesus Christ 69, 84, 88, 97, 101,
111, 133-134, 177; birth of 139;
church of 22, 27, 148, 193; com-
mission of 46, 170; confession
of 170; cornerstone 135-136,

163; disciples of 138; enemies
of 99; foundation 137; Gospel
of 75; Head of the church 64;
Lord 121; love of 76; merits of
81; and papacy 19, 25, 144, 161,
162; popularity of 15; and the
power of councils 66; Redeem-
er 122; righteousness of 93, 95;
the rock 29; sovereignty of 98;
teachings of 23, 140; vicar of 62,
67, 82, 123, 129, 130, 160, 165, 171,
172, 176; vicegerent of 144
Jews 15, 138-139
Joan of Arc 150
John 135, 136, 161-162
John, Bishop of Constantinople
168
John Paul II 133
John the Baptist 139
John IV of Constantinople 31
John VIII 55
John X 174
John XI 175
John XII 175
John XXII 175
John XXIII 128
Joseph II 115
Joseph of Arimathaea 138
Judas Iscariot 135, 176
Judea 135, 180
judgment 140, 152
Julius II 70, 169, 172
justification 90-93; by works 91
Justinian 167, 173
Justinian II, Emperor 53

Karlstadt 83
Kennedy, Ted 15

The Crisis of Our Time

HISTORIANS have christened the thirteenth century the Age of Faith and termed the eighteenth century the Age of Reason. The twentieth century was called many things: the Atomic Age, the Age of Inflation, the Age of the Tyrant, the Age of Aquarius. But the modern age deserves one name more than the others: the Age of Irrationalism. Contemporary intellectuals are anti-intellectual. Contemporary philosophers are anti-philosophy. Contemporary theologians are anti-theology.

In past centuries, secular philosophers have generally believed that knowledge is possible to man. Consequently they expended a great deal of thought and effort trying to justify their claims to know. In the twentieth century, however, the optimism of the secular philosophers all but disappeared. They despaired of knowing.

Like their secular counterparts, the great theologians and doctors of the church taught that knowledge is possible to man. Yet the theologians of the twentieth century repudiated that belief. They also despaired of knowledge. This radical skepticism has penetrated our entire culture, from television to music to literature. The Christian at the beginning of the twenty-first century is confronted with an overwhelming cultural consensus – sometimes stated explicitly but most often implicitly: Man does not and cannot know anything truly.

What does this have to do with Christianity? Simply this: If man can know nothing truly, man can truly know nothing. We cannot know that the Bible is the Word of God, that Christ died for his people, or that Christ is alive today at the right hand of the Father. Unless knowledge is possible, Christianity is nonsensical, for it claims to be knowledge. What is at stake at the beginning of the twenty-first century is not simply a single doctrine, such as the virgin birth, or the existence of Hell, as important as those doctrines may be, but the whole of Christianity itself. If knowledge is not possible to man, it is worse than silly to argue points of doctrine – it is insane.

The irrationalism of the present age is so thoroughgoing and pervasive that even the Remnant – the segment of the professing church that remains faithful – has accepted much of it, frequently without even being aware of what it is accepting. In some religious circles this irrationalism has become synonymous with piety and humility, and those who oppose it are denounced as rationalists, as though to be logical were a sin. Our contemporary anti-theologians make a contradiction and call it a Mystery. The faithful ask for truth and are given Paradox and Antinomy. If any resist swallowing the absurdities of the anti-theologians who teach in the seminaries or have graduated from the seminaries, they are frequently marked as heretics or schismatics who seek to act independently of God.

There is no greater threat facing the true church of Christ at this moment than the irrationalism that now controls our entire culture. Totalitarianism, guilty of hundreds of millions of murders – including those of millions of Christians – is to be feared, but not nearly so much as the idea that we do not and cannot know the literal truth. Hedonism, the popular philosophy of America, is not to be feared so much as the belief that logic – that "mere human logic," to use the religious irrationalists' own phrase – is futile. The attacks on truth, on knowledge, on propositional revelation, on the intellect, on words, and on logic are renewed daily. But note well: The misologists – the haters of logic – use logic to demonstrate the futility of using logic. The anti-intellectuals construct intricate intellectual arguments to prove the insufficiency of the intellect. Those who deny the competence of words to express thought use words to express their thoughts. The proponents of poetry, myth, metaphor, and analogy argue for their theories by using literal prose, whose competence – even whose possibility – they deny. The anti-theologians use the revealed Word of God to show that there can be no revealed Word of God – or that if there could, it would remain impenetrable darkness and Mystery to our finite minds.

Nonsense Has Come

Is it any wonder that the world is grasping at straws – the straws of experientialism, mysticism, and drugs? After all, if people are told that the Bible contains insoluble mysteries, then is not a flight into mysticism to be expected? On what grounds can it be condemned? Certainly not on logical grounds or Biblical grounds, if logic is futile and the Bible unintelligible. Moreover, if it cannot be condemned on logical or Biblical grounds, it cannot be condemned at all. If people are going to have a religion of the mysterious, they will not adopt Christianity: They will have a genuine mystery religion. The popularity of Roman Catholicism, Eastern mysticism, mind-altering drugs, and religious experience is the logical consequence of the irrationalism of the twentieth century. There can and will be no Christian reformation unless and until the irrationalism of the age is totally repudiated by Christians.

The Church Defenseless

Yet how shall they do it? The official spokesmen for Christianity have been fatally infected with irrationalism. The seminaries, which annually train thousands of men to teach millions of Christians, are the finishing schools of irrationalism, completing the job begun by government schools and colleges. Many of the pulpits of the conservative churches (we are not speaking of the obviously apostate churches) are occupied by graduates of the anti-theological schools. These products of modern anti-theological education, when asked to give a reason for the hope that is in them, can generally respond with only the vocal analogue of a shrug – a mumble about Mystery. They have not grasped – and therefore cannot teach those for whom they are responsible – the first truth: "And you shall know the truth." Many, in fact, explicitly deny it, saying that we can possess only "pointers" to the truth, or something "similar" to the truth, a mere analogy, but not the divine truth itself. Is the impotence of the Christian church a puzzle? Is the fascination with Pentecostalism, ritualism, faith healing, Eastern Orthodoxy, and Roman Catholicism – all sensate and anti-intellectual religions – among members of conservative churches an enigma? Not when one understands the pious nonsense that is purveyed in the name of God in the religious colleges and seminaries.

The Trinity Foundation

The creators of The Trinity Foundation firmly believe that theology is too important to be left to the licensed theologians – the graduates of the schools of theology. They have created The Trinity Foundation for the express purpose of teaching believers all that the Scriptures contain – not warmed over, baptized, non-Christian philosophies. Each member of the board of directors of The Trinity Foundation has signed this oath: "I believe that the Bible alone and the Bible in its entirety is the Word of God and, therefore, inerrant in the autographs. I believe that the system of truth presented in the Bible is best summarized in the *Westminster Confession of Faith*. So help me God."

The ministry of The Trinity Foundation is the presentation of the system of truth taught in Scripture as clearly and as completely as possible. We do not regard obscurity as a virtue, nor confusion as a sign of spirituality. Confusion, like all error, is sin, and teaching that confusion is all that Christians can hope for is doubly sin.

The presentation of the truth of Scripture necessarily involves the rejection of error. The Foundation has exposed and will continue to expose the irrationalism of the modern age, whether its current spokesman be an Existentialist philosopher or a professed Reformed theologian. We oppose anti-intellectualism, whether it be espoused by a Neo-orthodox theologian or a Fundamentalist evangelist. We reject misology, whether it be on the lips of a Neo-evangelical or those of a Roman Catholic Charismatic. We repudiate agnosticism, whether it be secular or religious. To each error we bring the brilliant light of Scripture, proving all things, and holding fast to that which is true.

The Primacy of Theory

The ministry of The Trinity Foundation is not a "practical" ministry. If you are a pastor, we will not enlighten you on how to organize an ecumenical prayer meeting in your community or how to double church attendance in a year. If you are a homemaker, you will have to read elsewhere to find out how to become a total woman. If you are a businessman, we will not tell you how to develop a social conscience. The professing church is drowning in such "practical" advice.

The Trinity Foundation is unapologetically theoretical in its outlook, believing that theory without practice is dead, and that practice without theory is blind. The trouble with the professing church is not primarily in its practice, but in its theory. Professing Christians and teachers do not know, and many do not even care to know, the doctrines of Scripture. Doctrine is intellectual, and professing Christians are generally anti-intellectual. Doctrine is ivory-tower philosophy, and they scorn ivory towers. The ivory tower, however, is the control tower of a civilization. It is a fundamental, theoretical mistake of the "practical" men to think that they can be merely practical, for practice is always the practice of some theory. The relationship between theory and practice is the relationship between cause and effect. If a person believes correct theory, his practice will tend to be correct. The practice of contemporary professing Christians is immoral because it is the practice of false theories. It is a major theoretical mistake of the "practical" men to think that they can ignore the ivory towers of the philosophers and theologians as irrelevant to their lives. Every action that "practical" men take is governed by the thinking that has occurred in some ivory tower – whether that tower be the British Museum; the Academy; a home in Basel, Switzerland; or a tent in Israel.

In Understanding Be Men

It is the first duty of the Christian to understand correct theory – correct doctrine – and thereby implement correct practice. This order – first theory, then practice – is both logical and Biblical. It is, for example, exhibited in Paul's *Epistle to the Romans*, in which he spends the first eleven chapters expounding theory and the last five discussing practice. The contemporary teachers of Christians have not only reversed the Biblical order, they have inverted the Pauline emphasis on theory and practice. The virtually complete failure of the teachers of the professing church to instruct believers in correct doctrine is the cause of the misconduct and spiritual and cultural impotence of Christians. The church's lack of power is the result of its lack of truth. The Gospel is the power of God, not religious experiences or personal relationships. The church has no power because it has abandoned the Gospel, the good news, for a religion of experientialism. Modern American Christians are children carried about by every wind of doctrine, not knowing what they believe, or even if they believe anything for certain.

The chief purpose of The Trinity Foundation is to counteract the irrationalism of the age and to expose the errors of the teachers of the church. Our emphasis – on the Bible as the sole source of knowledge, on the primacy of truth, on the supreme importance of correct doctrine, and on the necessity for systematic and logical thinking – is rare. To the extent that the church survives – and she will survive and flourish – it will be because of her increasing acceptance of these basic ideas and their logical implications.

We believe that The Trinity Foundation is filling a vacuum. We are saying that Christianity is intellectually defensible – that, in fact, it is the only intellectually defensible system of thought. We are saying that God has made the wisdom of this world – whether that wisdom be called science, religion, philosophy, or common sense – foolishness. We are appealing to all Christians who have not conceded defeat in the intellectual battle with the world to join us in our efforts to raise a standard to which all men of sound mind can repair.

The love of truth, of God's Word, has all but disappeared in our time. We are committed to and pray for a great instauration. But though we may not see this reformation in our lifetimes, we believe it is our duty to present the whole counsel of God because Christ has commanded it. The results of our teaching are in God's hands, not ours. Whatever those results, his Word is never taught in vain, but always accomplishes the result that he intended it to accomplish. Gordon H. Clark has stated our view well:

> There have been times in the history of God's people, for example, in the days of Jeremiah, when refreshing grace and widespread revival were not to be expected: The time was one of chastisement. If this twentieth century is of a similar nature, individual Christians here and there can find comfort and strength in a study of God's Word. But if God has decreed happier days for us, and if we may expect a world-shaking and genuine spiritual awakening, then it is the author's belief that a zeal for souls, however necessary, is not the sufficient condition. Have there not been devout saints in every age, numerous enough to carry on a revival? Twelve such persons are plenty. What distinguishes the arid ages from the period of the Reformation, when nations were moved as they had not been since Paul preached in Ephesus, Corinth, and Rome, is the latter's fullness of knowledge of God's Word. To echo an early Reformation thought, when the ploughman and the garage attendant know the Bible as well as the theologian does, and know it better than some contemporary theologians, then the desired awakening shall have already occurred.

In addition to publishing books, The Foundation publishes a monthly newsletter, *The Trinity Review*. Subscriptions to *The Review* are free to U.S. addresses; please write to the address on the book order form to become a subscriber. If you would like further information or would like to assist us in our work, please let us know.

The Trinity Foundation is a non-profit foundation, tax exempt under section 501 (c)(3) of the Internal Revenue Code of 1954. You can help us disseminate the Word of God through your tax-deductible contributions to The Foundation.

JOHN W. ROBBINS

Intellectual Ammunition

THE Trinity Foundation is committed to bringing every philosophical and theological thought captive to Christ. The books listed below are designed to accomplish that goal. They are written with two subordinate purposes: (1) to demolish all non-Christian claims to knowledge; and (2) to build a system of truth based upon the Bible alone.

Philosophy

Ancient Philosophy
Gordon H. Clark   Trade paperback $24.95
    This book covers the thousand years from the Pre-Socratics to Plotinus. It represents some of the early work of Dr. Clark – the work that made his academic reputation. It is an excellent college text.

Christ and Civilization
John W. Robbins   Trade paperback $5.95
    Civilization as we know it is a result of the widespread proclamation and belief of the Gospel of justification by faith alone in the sixteenth century. Christ foretold this result in the Sermon on the Mount: "Seek first the Kingdom of God and his righteousness, and all these things will be added to you." This brief overview of the history

of western civilization makes it clear that our cultural debt is to the Gospel, not to Greece and Rome.

Christian Philosophy   Hardback $29.95
Gordon H. Clark   Trade paperback $21.95
    This book, Volume 4 in *The Works of Gordon Haddon Clark*, combines three of his most important works in philosophy: *Three Types of Religious Philosophy*; *Religion, Reason and Revelation*; and *An Introduction to Christian Philosophy*. Together they constitute Dr. Clark's principal statement of his Christian philosophy.

A Christian Philosophy of Education   Hardback $18.95
Gordon H. Clark   Trade paperback $12.95
    The first edition of this book was published in 1946. It sparked interest in Christian schools. In the 1970s, Dr. Clark thoroughly revised and updated it, and it is needed now more than ever. Its chapters include: The Need for a World-View; The Christian World-View; The Alternative to Christian Theism; Neutrality; Ethics; The Christian Philosophy of Education; Academic Matters; and Kindergarten to University. Three appendices are included: The Relationship of Public Education to Christianity; A Protestant World-View; and Art and the Gospel. It is Volume 12 in *The Works of Gordon Haddon Clark*.

A Christian View of Men and Things   Hardback $29.95
Gordon H. Clark   Trade paperback $21.95
    No other book achieves what *A Christian View* does: the presentation of Christianity as it applies to history, politics, ethics, science, religion, and epistemology. Dr. Clark's command of both worldly philosophy and

Scripture is evident on every page, and the result is a breathtaking and invigorating challenge to the wisdom of this world. This is Volume 1 in *The Works of Gordon Haddon Clark.*

Clark and His Critics   Hardback $29.95
Gordon H. Clark   Trade paperback $21.95
    This book, Volume 7 in *The Works of Gordon Haddon Clark*, combines two separate books: *The Philosophy of Gordon H. Clark*, first published in 1968, and *Clark Speaks from the Grave*, first published in 1986. In this volume Clark answers all objections to his philosophy of Scripturalism and chides his critics for their incompetent defenses of the Christian faith. *Available 2008.*

Clark Speaks from the Grave
Gordon H. Clark   Trade paperback $3.95
    Dr. Clark chides some of his critics for their failure to defend Christianity competently. *Clark Speaks* is a stimulating and illuminating discussion of the errors of contemporary apologists.
    See also *Clark and His Critics.*

Ecclesiastical Megalomania:
The Economic and Political Thought
of the Roman Catholic Church   Hardback $29.95
John W. Robbins   Trade paperback $19.95
    This detailed and thorough analysis and critique of the social teaching of the Roman Church-State is the only such book available by a Christian economist and political philosopher. The book's conclusions reveal the

Roman Church-State to be an advocate of its own brand
of faith-based fascism. *Ecclesiastical Megalomania* includes the complete text of the *Donation of Constantine*
and Lorenzo Valla's exposé of the hoax.

Education, Christianity, and the State
J. Gresham Machen   Trade paperback $10.95
   Machen was one of the foremost educators, theologians,
and defenders of Christianity in the twentieth century.
The author of several scholarly books, Machen saw clearly
that if Christianity is to survive and flourish, a system of
Christian schools must be established. This collection of
essays and speeches captures his thoughts on education
over nearly three decades.

Essays on Ethics and Politics
Gordon H. Clark   Trade paperback $10.95
   Dr. Clark's essays, written over the course of five de-
cades, are a major statement of Christian ethics.

Freedom and Capitalism:
Essays on Christian Economics and Politics
John W. Robbins   Hardback $29.95
   The Biblical model for limited government and a free
society – the state the Holy Spirit describes in *Romans*
13 and 1 *Samuel* 8 – is despised by both Christians and
non-Christians, who think they have a moral mandate
to force others to be "charitable" and "Christian." This
book is a collection of 31 essays that defend *laissez-faire*
capitalism and constitutional government, the only moral
system of economics and government. Topics covered

include the draft, foreign policy, health care, taxation, monetary policy, faith-based welfare, the separation of church and state, and much more.

Gordon H. Clark: Personal Recollections
John W. Robbins, Editor   Trade paperback $6.95
 Friends of Dr. Clark have written their recollections of the man. Contributors include family members, colleagues, students, and friends such as Harold Lindsell, Carl Henry, Ronald Nash, and Anna Marie Hager.

Historiography: Secular and Religious
Gordon H. Clark   Trade paperback $13.95
 In this masterful work, Dr. Clark applies his philosophy to the writing of history, examining all the major schools of historiography.

Language and Theology
Gordon H. Clark   Trade paperback $9.95
 There were two main currents in twentieth-century philosophy – Language Philosophy and Existentialism. Both were hostile to Christianity. Dr. Clark disposes of Language Philosophy in this brilliant critique of Bertrand Russell, Ludwig Wittgenstein, Rudolf Carnap, A. J. Ayer, Langdon Gilkey, and many others.
 See also *Modern Philosophy.*

Logic
Gordon H. Clark   Hardback $16.95
 Written as a textbook for Christian schools, *Logic* is another unique book from Dr. Clark's pen. His presen-

tation of the laws of thought, which must be followed if Scripture is to be understood correctly, and which are found in Scripture itself, is both clear and thorough. *Logic* is an indispensable book for the thinking Christian.

Lord God of Truth, Concerning the Teacher
Gordon H. Clark, Aurelius Augustine Trade paperback $7.95
    This essay by Dr. Clark summarizes many of the most telling arguments against empiricism and defends the Biblical teaching that we know God and truth immediately. The dialogue by Augustine is a refutation of empirical language philosophy.

Modern Philosophy   Hardback $29.95
Gordon H. Clark   Trade paperback $21.95
    This book, Volume 5 in *The Works of Gordon Haddon Clark*, combines five separate books: *The Philosophy of Science and Belief in God*, *Behaviorism and Christianity*, *Language and Theology*, *William James*, and *John Dewey*. *Available 2008.*

The Philosophy of Science and Belief in God
Gordon H. Clark   Trade paperback $8.95
    In opposing the contemporary idolatry of science, Dr. Clark analyzes three major aspects of science: the problem of motion, Newtonian science, and modern theories of physics. His conclusion is that science, while it may be useful, is always false; and he demonstrates its falsity in numerous ways. Since science is always false, it can offer no credible alternative to the Bible and Christianity.
    See also *Modern Philosophy.*

The Scripturalism of Gordon H. Clark
W. Gary Crampton   Trade paperback $9.95
    Dr. Crampton has written an introduction to the
philosophy of Gordon H. Clark that is helpful to both
beginners and advanced students of theology. This book
includes a bibliography of Dr. Clark's works.

Thales to Dewey: A History of Philosophy   Hardback $29.95
Gordon H. Clark   Trade paperback $21.95
    This is the best one-volume history of philosophy in
print. It is Volume 3 in *The Works of Gordon Haddon
Clark.*

William James and John Dewey
Gordon H. Clark   Trade paperback $8.95
    William James and John Dewey are two of the most
influential philosophers America has produced. Their
philosophies of Instrumentalism and Pragmatism are
hostile to Christianity, and Dr. Clark demolishes their
arguments.
    See also *Modern Philosophy.*

Without A Prayer: Ayn Rand and the Close of Her System
John W. Robbins   Trade paperback $19.95
    Ayn Rand has been a best-selling author since 1957.
Without A Prayer discusses Objectivism's epistemology,
theology, ethics, and politics in detail. Appendices include
analyses of books by Leonard Peikoff and David Kelley, as
well as several essays on Christianity and philosophy.

Theology

Against the Churches: The Trinity Review 1989-1998
John W. Robbins, Editor   Oversize hardback $39.95
   This is the second volume of 77 essays from *The Trinity Review*, covering its second ten years, 1989-1998. This volume, like the first, is fully indexed and is very useful in research and in the classroom. Authors include Gordon Clark, Charles Hodge, J. C. Ryle, Horatius Bonar, and Robert L. Dabney.

Against the World: The Trinity Review 1978-1988
John W. Robbins, Editor   Oversize hardback $34.95
   This is a clothbound collection of the essays published in *The Trinity Review* from 1978 to 1988, 70 in all. Fully indexed, it is a valuable source of information and arguments explaining and defending Christianity.

The Atonement
Gordon H. Clark   Trade paperback $8.95
   In *The Atonement,* Dr. Clark discusses the covenants, the virgin birth and incarnation, federal headship and representation, the relationship between God's sovereignty and justice, and much more. He analyzes traditional views of the atonement and criticizes them in the light of Scripture alone.

The Biblical Doctrine of Man
Gordon H. Clark   Trade paperback $6.95
   Is man soul and body or soul, spirit, and body? What is the image of God? Is Adam's sin imputed to his children? Is evolution true? Are men totally depraved? What is the

heart? These are some of the questions discussed and answered from Scripture in this book.

By Scripture Alone
W. Gary Crampton   Trade paperback $12.95
    This is a clear and thorough explanation of the Scriptural doctrine of Scripture and a refutation of the recent Romanist attack on Scripture as the Word of God.

Can the Orthodox Presbyterian Church Be Saved?
John W. Robbins   Trade paperback $3.95
    This small book, which demonstrates the central errors of OPC history and theology since the 1940s, is an alarm to awaken members of the OPC from their slumbers.

The Changing of the Guard
Mark W. Karlberg   Trade paperback $3.95
    This essay is a critical discussion of Westminster Seminary's anti-Reformational and un-Biblical teaching on the doctrine of justification. Dr. Karlberg exposes the doctrine of justification by faith and works – not *sola fide* – taught at Westminster Seminary for the past 30 years, by Professors Norman Shepherd, Richard Gaffin, John Frame, and others.

Christianity and Neo-Liberalism: The Spiritual Crisis in the Orthodox Presbyterian Church and Beyond
Paul M. Elliott   Trade paperback $19.95
    This massively-documented book details the influence Westminster Theological Seminary has had on the Orthodox Presbyterian Church and other churches and

organizations. It is both a work of theological analysis and a call to action.

The Church Effeminate
John W. Robbins, Editor   Hardback $29.95

   This is a collection of 39 essays by the best theologians of the church on the doctrine of the church: Martin Luther, John Calvin, Benjamin Warfield, Gordon Clark, J. C. Ryle, and many more. The essays cover the structure, function, and purpose of the church.

The Clark-Van Til Controversy
Herman Hoeksema   Trade paperback $9.95

   This collection of essays by the founder of the Protestant Reformed Churches – essays written at the time of the Clark-Van Til controversy in the 1940s – is one of the best commentaries on those events in print.

A Companion to The Current Justification Controversy
John W. Robbins   Trade paperback $9.95

   This book includes documentary source material not available in *The Current Justification Controversy*, an essay tracing the origins and continuation of this controversy throughout American Presbyterian churches, and an essay on the New Perspective on Paul by Robert L. Reymond.

Cornelius Van Til: The Man and The Myth
John W. Robbins   Trade paperback $2.45

   The actual teachings of this eminent Philadelphia theologian have been obscured by the myths that surround him. This book penetrates those myths and criticizes Van Til's surprisingly unorthodox views of God and the Bible.

Counterfeit Miracles: A Defense of Divine Miracles
Against Pagan, Medieval, and Modern Marvels
Benjamin B. Warfield   Trade paperback $19.95
    This book contains the 1918 lectures delivered by Professor Warfield of Princeton Seminary. It is more timely today than it was 90 years ago.

The Current Justification Controversy
O. Palmer Robertson   Trade paperback $9.95
    From 1975 to 1982 a controversy over justification raged within Westminster Theological Seminary and the Philadelphia Presbytery of the Orthodox Presbyterian Church. As a member of the faculties of both Westminster and Covenant Seminaries during this period, O. Palmer Robertson was an important participant in this controversy. This is his account of the controversy, vital background for understanding the defection from the Gospel that is now widespread in American Presbyterian churches.

In Defense of Theology
Gordon H. Clark   Trade paperback $9.95
    In this book Dr. Clark addresses several groups of people who oppose Christian theology: atheists, the Neo-orthodox, and the Uninterested. All three hold a common opinion: Truth and theology have nothing to do with each other. Dr. Clark demonstrates that theology is truth, and as thoroughly intellectual as astrophysics – and a lot less speculative.

God and Evil: The Problem Solved
Gordon H. Clark   Trade paperback $5.95
This volume is Chapter 5 of *Religion, Reason and Revelation*, in which Dr. Clark presents the Biblical solution to the problem of evil.

God-Breathed: The Divine Inspiration of the Bible
Louis Gaussen   Trade paperback $16.95
Gaussen, a nineteenth-century Swiss Reformed pastor, comments on hundreds of passages in which the Bible claims to be the Word of God. This is a massive defense of the doctrine of the plenary and verbal inspiration of Scripture.

God's Hammer: The Bible and Its Critics
Gordon H. Clark   Trade paperback $10.95
The starting point of Christianity, the doctrine on which all other doctrines depend, is "The Bible alone, and the Bible in its entirety, is the Word of God written, and, therefore, inerrant in the autographs." Over the centuries the opponents of Christianity, with Satanic shrewdness, have concentrated their attacks on the truthfulness and completeness of the Bible. In the twentieth century the attack was not so much in the fields of history and archaeology as in philosophy. Dr. Clark's brilliant defense of the complete truthfulness of the Bible is captured in this collection of eleven major essays.

The Holy Spirit
Gordon H. Clark   Trade paperback $8.95
This discussion of the third person of the Trinity is both concise and exact. Dr. Clark includes chapters on the work of the Spirit, sanctification, and Pentecostalism.

The Incarnation
Gordon H. Clark   Trade paperback $8.95
  Who is Christ? The attack on the doctrine of the Incarnation in the nineteenth and twentieth centuries was
vigorous, but the orthodox response was lame. Dr. Clark
reconstructs the doctrine of the Incarnation, building
and improving upon the Chalcedonian definition.

The Johannine Logos
Gordon H. Clark   Trade paperback $5.95
  Dr. Clark analyzes the relationship between Christ,
who is the truth, and the Bible. He explains why John
used the same word to refer to both Christ and his
teaching. Chapters deal with the Prologue to John's
Gospel; *Logos* and *Rheemata*; Truth; and Saving Faith.
See also *What Is Saving Faith?*

Karl Barth's Theological Method
Gordon H. Clark   Trade paperback $18.95
  Karl Barth's Theological Method is perhaps the best
critique of the Neo-orthodox theologian Karl Barth
ever written. Dr. Clark discusses Barth's view of revelation, language, and Scripture, focusing on his method
of writing theology, rather than presenting a comprehensive analysis of the details of Barth's theology.

Logical Criticisms of Textual Criticism
Gordon H. Clark   Trade paperback $3.25
  Dr. Clark's acute mind enables him to demonstrate the
inconsistencies, assumptions, and flights of fancy that
characterize the science of New Testament criticism.
See also *Commentaries on Paul's Letters.*

Not Reformed at All: Medievalism in "Reformed" Churches
John Robbins and Sean Gerety   Trade paperback $9.95
This book is a response to and refutation of Douglas
Wilson's book *"Reformed" Is Not Enough: Recovering the*
Objectivity of the Covenant. Wilson, one of the leading
figures in the Neolegalist movement in Reformed and
Presbyterian circles, attacked covenant theology and
proposed a "visible, photographable" covenant that one
enters by ritual baptism, making one a Christian. Wilson's
"salvation" can be lost by one's own lackluster perfor-
mance or nullified by actions of authorized representatives of the organized church. This refutation of Wilson
is a defense of the Gospel and the Covenant of Grace.

Not What My Hands Have Done
Charles Hodge, Horatius Bonar   Trade paperback $16.95
This is the combined edition of *Justification by Faith*
Alone (by Hodge) and *The Everlasting Righteousness* (by
Bonar). Combined, these books offer both an introduc-
tion to and an in-depth discussion of the central doctrine
of Christianity, justification by faith alone.

Papal Power: Its Origins and Development
Henry T. Hudson   Trade paperback $12.95
The origins and growth of an absolute monarchy
claiming to be the only genuine church of Jesus Christ is
a story few Christians know – to their great danger and
detriment. This monograph is an excellent discussion
of the totalitarian Roman Catholic Church-State in the
Middle Ages, and its flourishing in the 21st Century.

Predestination
Gordon H. Clark   Trade paperback $12.95
   Dr. Clark thoroughly discusses one of the most controversial and pervasive doctrines of the Bible: that God is,
quite literally, Almighty. Free will, the origin of evil, God's
omniscience, creation, and the new birth are all presented
within a Scriptural framework. The objections of those
who do not believe in Almighty God are considered and
refuted. This edition also contains the text of the booklet,
Predestination in the Old Testament.

Sacramental Sorcery: The Invalidity
of Roman Catholic Baptism
James H. Thornwell   Trade paperback $12.95
   In 1845 the General Assembly of the American Presbyterian Church declared that Roman Catholic baptism is
not Christian baptism. Its almost unanimous decision
was immediately attacked by Charles Hodge of Prince-
ton Seminary. Thornwell wrote this defense of the 1845
decision, and Hodge never published a reply. Thornwell's
book still stands today, 160 years later, as the unrefuted
argument demonstrating the invalidity of Roman Catholic baptism. This book is must reading for all Christians,
especially for those proclaiming the Gospel to Roman
Catholics.

Sanctification
Gordon H. Clark   Trade paperback $8.95
   In this book Dr. Clark discusses historical theories of
sanctification, the sacraments, and the Biblical doctrine
of sanctification.

Slavery and Christianity: Paul's Letter to Philemon
John W. Robbins   Trade paperback $6.95
    For centuries the Bible has been twisted into a defense
of slavery, but Paul's letter to the slaveholder Philemon is
clearly a document endorsing freedom. Onesimus returns
to Philemon "no longer as a slave," but as a free man.

Study Guide to the Westminster Confession
W. Gary Crampton   Oversize paperback $10.95
    This *Study Guide* can be used by individuals or classes.
It contains a paragraph-by-paragraph summary of the
Westminster Confession, and questions for the student to
answer. Space for answers is provided. The *Guide* will be
most beneficial when used in conjunction with Dr. Clark's
What Do Presbyterians Believe?

A Theology of the Holy Spirit
Frederick Dale Bruner   Trade paperback $16.95
    First published in 1970, this book has been hailed by
reviewers as "thorough," "fair," "comprehensive," "devas-
tating," "the most significant book on the Holy Spirit,"
and "scholarly." Gordon Clark described this book in his
own book *The Holy Spirit* as "a masterly and exceedingly
well researched exposition of Pentecostalism. The docu-
mentation is superb, as is also his penetrating analysis
of their non-Scriptural and sometimes contradictory
conclusions." Unfortunately, the book is marred by the
author's sacramentarianism.

The Trinity
Gordon H. Clark   Trade paperback $8.95
   Apart from the doctrine of Scripture, no teaching
of the Bible is more fundamental than the doctrine of
God. Dr. Clark's defense of the orthodox doctrine of the
Trinity is a principal portion of his systematic theology.
There are chapters on the Deity of Christ; Augustine; the
Incomprehensibility of God; Bavinck and Van Til; and
the Holy Spirit; among others.

What Calvin Says
W. Gary Crampton   Trade paperback $10.95
   This is a clear, readable, and thorough introduction to
the theology of John Calvin.

What Do Presbyterians Believe?
Gordon H. Clark   Trade paperback $10.95
   This classic is the best commentary on the *Westminster
Confession of Faith* ever written.

What Is Saving Faith?
Gordon H. Clark   Trade paperback $12.95
   This is the combined edition of *Faith and Saving Faith*
and *The Johannine Logos.* The views of the Roman Catholic Church, John Calvin, Thomas Manton, John Owen,
Charles Hodge, and B. B. Warfield are discussed in this
book. Is the object of faith a person or a proposition? Is
faith more than belief? Is belief thinking with assent, as
Augustine said? In a world chaotic with differing views of
faith, Dr. Clark clearly explains the Biblical view of faith
and saving faith.

In *The Johannine Logos*, Dr. Clark analyzes the relationship between Christ, who is the truth, and the Bible. He explains why John used the same word to refer to both Christ and his teaching. Chapters deal with the Prologue to John's *Gospel*; *Logos* and *Rheemata*; Truth; and Saving Faith.

Clark's Commentaries on the New Testament

Colossians	Trade paperback	$6.95
Commentaries on Paul's Letters		
(*Colossians, Ephesians, 1* and		
2 Thessalonians, Logical		
Criticisms of Textual	Hardback	$29.95
Criticism)	Trade paperback	$21.95
First Corinthians	Trade paperback	$10.95
First John	Trade paperback	$10.95
New Heavens, New Earth		
(*First and Second Peter*)	Trade paperback	$10.95
The Pastoral Epistles	Hardback	$29.95
(*1* and *2 Timothy and Titus*)	Trade paperback	$21.95
Philippians	Trade paperback	$9.95

All of Dr. Clark's commentaries are expository, not technical, and are written for the Christian layman. His purpose is to explain the text clearly and accurately so that the Word of God will be thoroughly known by every Christian.

The Trinity Library

We will send you one copy of each of the 65 books listed above for $600 (retail value $900), postpaid to any address in the United States. You may also order the books you want individually on the order form on the next page. Because some of the books are in short supply, we must reserve the right to substitute others of equal or greater value in The Trinity Library. This special offer expires October 31, 2010.

Order Form

NAME _____

ADDRESS _____

TELEPHONE _____

E-MAIL _____

❑ Please add my name to the mailing list. (You may also enter your email address at our website to receive special notices from The Foundation.)

❑ Please accept this gift for your work $_____. (All donations to The Trinity Foundation are tax-deductible to the fullest extent of the law.)

❑ Please send me _____ additional copies of *Papal Power.* I enclose as payment U.S. $_____.

❑ Please send me the Trinity Library of 65 books. I enclose U.S. $600 as full payment.

❑ Please send me the following books. I enclose full payment in the amount of U.S. $_____ for them.

_____

_____

_____

_____

The Trinity Foundation
Post Office Box 68
Unicoi, Tennessee 37692

Website: www.trinityfoundation.org
423.743.0199

Shipping: Please add $6.00 for the first book and 75 cents for each additional book. Foreign addresses: Please add $15.00 for the first book and $5.00 for each additional book. Books will be shipped by air to foreign addresses.